NIGGER
101

(The Basic Nigger Lesson Plan)

The Truth! The Whole Truth! And Nothing But The Truth!

About The Word Nigger And Them Niggers

The Plain, Simple Truth, In Black And White, To Heal Our Souls

By Mustafa Rasul Al-Amin

Created In 2006 "As A Bootleg Book" by Three Brothers Publishing

"Bismillah"

(The Name Of The Creator Is Invoked Upon This Project)

"The Afrikan Assassination"

A planned devastation,
A destructive calculation,
The occupation and assassination of an Afrikan nation,
Through assimilation, miseduKKKation, incarceration and isolation!
Why doesn't your observation reveal an Afrikan assassination of calculation?

"Mustafa Rasul Al-Amin"
(091495)

Dedication.......

This compilation of liberation essays is sincerely dedicated to my dear Brothers Shelby Lanier Junior, and Osagyefo K. Nkrumah (a.k.a. Jimmie T. "JT" Woods). You are two of the most influential and inspirational brothers that I have ever had the pleasure of being acquainted.

Each time The Creator has blessed me to be in the presence of you two spiritual warriors; I can't help but visualize the Afrikan versions of Romulus and Remus. As I visualize you, as two valiant Afrikan war gods leading invincible Afrikan armies into war and onto the battlefield, defiantly confronting the racial injustices and racist tyrannies that have plagued our people from the beginnings of recorded time. You are unsung, heroic foot Souljahs who constantly march, tirelessly, and relentlessly, day after day, proudly standing on the front lines of unjust battlefields, valiantly fighting to protect and serve in the interests' of our people.

From One Souljah To Another.......

You are inspirations and role models for us all and to us all. In the Swahili spirit from this day forward you shall be baptized in the Swahili spirit, and your Swahili names are now revealed. Respectively, the spirits of the Swahili ancestors have revealed your names as Mkuu wa Jeshi (Chief of The Army), and Mkuu wa Askari (Chief Souljah).

Mkuu wa Jeshi – Chief of The Army (Shelby Lanier Junior)

Since long before I encountered you on the battlefields, you were one of my most admired heroes. From afar, I watched you as you attempted to shake the very foundations of the oppressors' establishment. At one time, as a young child, I thought you were the national leader of the Black Panther Party. I observed you; absolutely amazed at your strength and courageousness, as you confronted the racist powers, which dared rise up against our people. You are the inspiration within me that inspires me, and strengthens me, and commands me to keep being me!

I literally watched you, waiting for the fire to come flaring from your nostrils, and thunder and lightening in your heart and soul to explode from of your eyes and spew from your lips, instantaneously destroying our enemies! So much for childhood fantasies (smile). Your thunderous words helped to inspire, shape, and create this book. Your inflammable spirit forever keeps lit the eternal torch which burns so brightly in my soul!

Mkuu wa Askari – Chief Souljah (Osagyefo K. Nkrumah a.k.a. JT Woods)

Previous to meeting you, people repeatedly told me that it was imperative that we meet, due to our similar ideologies. They spoke of you as if you were royalty; a wealthy African King, with tons of precious metals and jewels which filled your coffers. And, as people were literally approaching me to meet you, for awhile it seemed as if you were some sort of apparition; for each time I would come to a place, it would soon be learned that you had just left. When I finally did meet you, it was at the African Ball. Needless to say my Brother, "I was awestruck!" There stood "The Mighty O," in all his glorious Afrikan regalia.

There you stood, completely decked out, in the most regal Afrikan ceremonial dress I had ever witnessed. Everyone kept telling me, "That's Mr. Woods, go talk to him." In my thinking and according to protocol, no one approaches royalty, unless an audience has been requested. You are the spiritually rich Afrikan King that so many made you out to be. For me, you will forever be Osagyefo, *Mkuu wa Askari,* The Mighty O! You strengthen me, you inspire me, and you encourage me O! You are a great source of my power O.

Mkuu WA Jeshi and Mkuu WA Askari this book, this weapon is my gift to you!

Your Dear Brother, Mustafa Rasul Al-Amin (Mkuu wa Rasullah – The Messenger)

What's Happening Baby?

The Killing Of Niggers Became An Acceptably Pleasurable Social Event

Definition.......

Niggerology - 1 a: the branch of knowledge concerning the creation, examination, study, research, affects and effect of phenomenon known as nigger(s)

b: The laws and phenomenon relating to the word nigger, or to the human reconstruction and transformation of people into nigger(s)

2 a: the science concerning the study of the nigger(s) psychiatry, psychology, sociology and the behaviors in relation to a particular field of knowledge or activity.

b; regarding, about, concerning in relation to or pertaining to nigger(s)

3. The Willie Lynch curriculum (methods/tactics)

Niggerology –

1. a: The secret, racially motivated division of science that pertains to the creation of, the examination of, the experimentation of, the manipulation of, the influences on and the influencing of, and the end results of the word nigger; the man-made being called nigger, and the psychological nigger behaviors inculcated into people of Afrikan descent, for the purposes of evolutionary manipulation.

b: The laws and phenomenon relating to the psychological and physical creation, and manipulation of niggers as individuals and, as a group.

c: The physical and psychological study of creating nigger mentalities and behaviors in correlation to a particular field of study, knowledge, or activity.

d: The science concerning niggers.

2. The creation, examination, manipulation and study of niggers a.k.a. niggas**.**

3. The Willie Lynch curriculum (The Willie Lynch training methods and tactics)

(About The Cover)

The racist people, who care least about us in this entire world, constantly create derogatory images of us, depicting us as creatures of buffoonery, and low intelligence, to put on display for the entire world. They then teach us that, "imitations are a form of flattery" and we begin to accept and imitate, and become their dysfunctional definitions. In reality they are ridiculing us and reinforcing their fictitious justifications for our incarceration and extermination. In reality, they despised us so much that, they wouldn't even let our real faces be freely broadcast in their movies or on their televisions. Now that's some real hatred! Caucasian people in blackface often depicted Africans; "cooning" for the cameras.

Note: The letter C (representing color) has been consciously removed from the words Afrika and Afrikan, and has been replaced with the letter K (which stands representative of knowledge).

"Mustafa Rasul Al-Amin"
(2006)

Introduction.......

Every dream starts with an idea,
Every idea starts with a thought,
And every, inspirational thought,
Is a Divinely inspirational seed;
Planted by "The Divine Creator"

"Mustafa Rasul Al-Amin"
(Monday, September 4, 2006)

The Creator of all things has deeply sewn seeds into the very depths of my soul, to be cultivated, nurtured and grown. Divine seeds, which are intended to produce fruit that will both restore to health, and defend against the destructive and detrimental effects, of an unhealthy and immoral diet, which most Afrikans are being premeditatedly, purposefully, and unsympathetically instructed (and forced) to consume.

The oppressive enemies of Afrikan people world-wide, daily feed us in calculated, measured doses; sinful diets high in negativity constructed upon foundations of nigger ideologies in attempts to create detrimental and destructive, counterfeit nigger realities. Faux, fictional, nigger realities calculated to transform Afrikan personalities into nigger personalities, which are centered in, and based upon the destructively counterfeit false foundations of immorality, depravation and wickedness. Daily, Blacks surrender to wicked fallacies, which are carefully crafted to look like and reflect in duality the nigger mentalities, and nigger immoralities, which are carefully crafted to be viewed as virtuous, advantageous and most important; Black normalities.

These divine seeds have resulted in this divine fruit; being written with the intention of being disseminated to all Afrikan people first and foremost, in an effort to demonstrate the dangers in accepting and becoming the nigger descriptive, that our enslavers, and our oppressors have so *thoughtfully,* designed for us. This book is to be utilized as a weapon, and a teaching tool against the racist miseduKKKation of the Negro in AmeriKKKa and the world. The foremost objective of this book is to enlighten, instruct, demonstrate and communicate to our people, the negative ramifications of submitting to the ignorant rationalizations of the racists' xenophobes, which most often shape our cultures, define us as a people, and control our futures.

It has long been a successful subterfuge of war to, "divide and conquer." Just as the old aphorism warns us, "Together We Stand, Divided We Fall." Afrikans must become a people united! Afrikans must begin to stand strong together. Afrikans must begin to understand that word nigger, is a divisive, conflict-ridden curse word, which in its very contrivance; it is intended to "divide and conquer" Afrikan people!

Daily, we witness self-professed niggers and niggas renouncing and denouncing any and all connections, with people of Afrikan ancestry. Daily, we witness the unreasonable self-hatred, of self-professed niggers and niggas who spew forth and regurgitate some of the most bigoted, vile and vicious, racial epithets and stereotypes to ever be uttered; inward toward their own selves and their own Afrikan people. Renouncing and denouncing their own Afrikan ancestry, aiming their learned hatred and detestation of Afrikan people, back at their same Afrikan selves, demeaning their own Afrikan ancestors, from whom we are derivatives.

Some very close to me have suggested that, maybe the title and cover of this book should be toned down and changed to be more socially correct. They've suggested that I use euphemisms like, "The N-Word" in place of nigger and nigga. These suggestions (and demands) were sincerely thought, out and discussed.

The Divine Creator planted seeds within me in their rawest form. Our enemies use the nigger curse in its crudest and most rudimentary form. *"Niggerology 101"* is a declaration of war against their evil! The time has come for us to bring it as hard as, or even harder than our enemies bring it to us! The time has come for us to discuss and address this contagion in its rawest and truest form. It is long past the time for us to pull the covers off niggers and expose those niggas; and to hold everything, and *every-body* accountable!

Daily, that abominable word, "nigger," is tossed around with more and more casualness, and daily, those of us for whom this word was fashioned and intended; descend deeper and deeper into the destructively demoralizing depths of despair, despondency and desperation; suffering dubious deaths, and destruction.

Unbeknownst to most, Afrikans are the deliberate, and the intentional targets of their wicked abomination. Nigger is an iniquitous incantation, designed by malevolent people, to lead Afrikan people into the throes damnation, devastation and ruination, upon its very invocation! Certain vocalizations possess enormous amounts of power, for the spoken word is a very influential medium. The words we speak, constructed in deliberately premeditated patterns, can lead us to hope, health, and happiness, or death, destruction, and despair. The word nigger is an evil word fashioned from the depths evil to constantly produce, reproduce and broadcast the wickedness that nigger encompasses. The word nigger; possesses that much power!

This book/lesson plan is a tutorial of essays, observations and poetry intended to assist in the stimulation, education and revitalization of the Afrikan mind, body and soul. This volume is being written as a heartfelt effort, to guide back the innumerable multitudes of Afrikans, who have naively succumbed to the carefully crafted deceptions of bigoted oppressors. This book/lesson plan is being written especially for those who *think* that they can change definitions; by endeavoring to put positive spins on sin. "Where are my niggas at?" They're lost, within AmeriKKKa's ghettoes, jails, penitentiaries, and those prisons of their own minds!

Brothers! Far too frequently we sit back like pathetic men, continuously losing immeasurable numbers of our very own sons, daughters, nephews and nieces to those murderous streets, the injustice systems and eternally; to cold funeral homes. We are fundamentally losing family because, "We have surrendered and are daily surrendering to their curse of nigger!" Far too many of them think that they can make nigger into a positive. There is no positive spin on sin. Sin is intended to be conquered and shunned, not embraced and spun. Iniquity ignorantly embraced and spun frequently produces violently ignorant niggas with guns.

AmeriKKKa long ago initiated her unconstructive paradigm to fabricate niggers, and construct faux nigger realities, and the slaves have long since fallen prey to their nigger agendas. AmeriKKKa produces nigger music, nigger movies, nigger fashions and a host of the nigger things, for them niggers and niggas to do. Our oppressors have fashioned paradoxical nigger paradigms, premeditated to by design, to function on the basic principles of, "trust, trick, and trap." They encourage Blacks to ***trust*** those people who enslaved and oppressed them; and ***trick*** them into falling for their forged fallacies, and dreams of being prosperous niggers, getting nigger rich; and ***trap*** niggers, into the never-ending cycles of, forever chasing superficial shadows and those faux fantasies which are designed to eviscerate, incarcerate, and annihilate niggers.

Culture is the foundation of any prosperous people. As Afrikans we have lots of cultures rich in traditions, well heeled in histories, and flourishing in successes. Look at our oppressors. They're always falling back on and espousing their different ethnic cultures. Yet, when we carefully investigate much of their cultural history, we discover that many of the honorable aspects of their cultures are robbed from others' cultures. People! Never renounce your own culture! From the time we first disembarked upon Amerikkka's shores as slaves, the racists repeatedly attempted to strip us of even the slightest memories our culture. Richard Pryor once told us that the judge once said to him, "You got any dreams nigger? We want them too!"

The racist culture vultures are continuously forcing manufactured counterfeit cultures upon Afrikans. First they fashioned a slave culture; as an Afrikan reality. Next they produced various forms of Negro cultures, manufacturing submissive, docile realities, for the purpose of controlling the thoughts and actions of Black people. And now, we find them once again, pulling the strings that create and manipulate Black cultures. Quite often, in Black face; the racist induce upon us hip-hop cultures and gangster cultures. Counterfeit misogynistic realities which celebrate homicide, fratricide, criminality, promiscuity, death and destruction! More nigger (nigga) cultures for the slave! Let us be Afrikans not niggers! Let us be Souljahs, not slaves!

This is being written for those countless, faceless, millions who have been misinformed by the oppressive manipulators of racists' societies. This book is being written to protect all people from those same people whose fundamental intentions are to eviscerate, dominate, incarcerate and eradicate Afrikans world wide!

"It is time for class my people! So, let the lessons begin."

(Chapter One)

"TRUTH"
(Can You Handle It?)

Truth – *(1) In accordance with fact or reality (2) Genuine; rightly or strictly so called; not spurious or counterfeit; exact; accurate; without variation*

"Did The Truth Cause These People To Do This?"

For many people, and especially for Afrikan people in America, truth can be an untrustworthy and in many instances, a very complex, and difficult complication to understand. Understanding that; for way too long, Afrikan people have been purposely and purposefully misinformed to the detriment of the entire race. We then recognize that far too often and for too long Afrikan people have been lied to, lied on, and lied about.

Many centuries before those first Afrikan kidnap victims were so callously dragged, kicking and screaming through the jungles, and through those gloomily damnable, "Doors of No Return," on Afrika's West Coast, by their iniquitous kidnappers and enslavers; systems of fabricated realities had already been created, for the sole purposes of conquering Afrika, and controlling, enslaving, defeating, and destroying Afrikans.

Iniquitous, pseudo realisms, and specious ideologies were already being falsely fabricated, and fashioned for generations of bamboozled Afrikans to exist in. Artificial realities were carefully crafted for the purpose of capturing, controlling, enslaving and killing Afrikans. Counterfeit realities were condescendingly crafted to create niggers, and to make Afrikans pathetically apathetic, pathologically unconscionable, completely unconscious, and absolutely blissful. Victims are blissfully ignorant to the actual realisms of real of truths.

The deceitfulness of Afrikan enslavers, Afrikan murderers, Afrikan oppressors, and the untrustworthiness of Afrikan parents, have been carried on for so long, that for many of us now; we either don't possess the knowledge of truth, lack a comprehensive understanding of actual truth, or we lack the courage, and the wisdom to straightforwardly acknowledge and accept the realities and consequences of authentic truths.

Afrikans have been misled for so long; many simply do not recognize or understand actual truth or reality.

Afrikan people for far too long have been deliberately and erroneously taught that, when we are trying to discover the absolute truth of a matter, it is possible to agree to disagree, and still ascertain the truth, the whole truth and nothing but the truth. One contemporary aphorism among Afrikan people and especially Afrikan preachers is, "We all have to learn to agree to disagree." This lie is not only an illogical statement, but it is a foolishly unconstructive and dangerously destructive declaration and principle; for any to live by.

Too many people think that there can be many variations of the truth, as it pertains to the same essential subject matter. Too many believe that variations of truths, are still the absolute truth, the whole truth, and nothing but the truth. Even though, their versions of the truth may significantly conflict in the basic nature, or definition with one another, many will tell us, "You can have your truths, they can have their truths, and we can all have, and keep our own different truths, even when it concerns to the same subject matters, or involves resolving clear-cut problems, which concern us all. They tell us that we can all agree to disagree even when there is but one specific answer, to a very unambiguous and specific problem.

In other words, some could say that our people are Black; they say that our people are Negro; we can say that our people are Afrikan; others could say that our people are coloreds; our enslavers, and oppressors could rename our people nigger and still others could say that our people are dark-skinned people, brown people, or niggas. In truth; are there in fact any differences between Afrikans, Blacks, coloreds, Negroes, niggas and niggers? How do we agree to disagree and rediscover our true racial and cultural identities?

As we can see from the preceding paragraph, each descriptive word presents a different rendering of our people, which either vaguely, or tremendously redefines our people, and for many of them, the questions still remain, "Who are we, what are we and from whence did we come?" The predicament of learning our true racial and cultural identities becomes bogged down in the muck and mire of unnecessary semantics.

Why not approach our conversations conscientiously; rationally seeking solutions, and all come out with a single, simple, uncomplicated, straightforward descriptive? Why couldn't we say, "Today, Afrikan peoples have discovered that we are the descendants of Afrikan peoples so, we will logically be; Afrikan people?"

Some may ask, "Why can't we all see the one truth?" Simply put, *"our pride."* Everybody wants to be the right one. Hence, our arrogance, our conceit, our smugness, our self-importance, and our self-righteous egos blind so many to the truth. Furthermore, the zillions of deceptions, created for each of us, reinforce our pride, and in turn tremendously increases the depths our blindness.

Due to our pride, many refuse to see, refuse to understand, or even refuse to acknowledge that real truth is not and cannot be based upon faith, sociological ideologies, superstitions, or religious beliefs. Instead, truth must have a foundation which is based in factual evidences, logical deductions, and truthful realities. Anything that stands in conflict or opposition to the truth is in truth nothing more, than a falsehood.

When people gather together to discuss their concerns or to find the truth of a matter, in attempts to make progress as a people, it is imperative that they attend the meeting with open-minds. If everyone comes to the meeting with self-centered motives, hidden agendas, their own egotistical realities, or the thoughtless preconceived notions of agreeing to disagree; then the meeting, and the subsequent discussions shall be doomed pointless, and will assuredly prove to be fruitless. Open minds and open hearts are a necessity!

The participants of the conference, as well as those expected to be served, will be forever trapped in their own selfish, self-centered quagmires, at the end of each conference, at the end of each day, at the end of each month, at the end of each year, and ultimately, at the end of each and every lifetime; our people will be forever trapped in those premeditated deceptions and lies designed by our oppressors for the purpose of destroying Afrikans! Racists' lies are intentionally fashioned to purposely dehumanize Afrikan people.

Many of the dysfunctional rituals practiced by Black people today and witnessed by the world are in reality evolutionary by-products of countless deceptions *"sold"* to generations past. We must acknowledge truth.

Al-Quran Surah 13 Ayats 18 and 19

18: And turn not thy face away from people in contempt, nor go about in the land exultingly.
Surely Allah loves not a self-conceited boaster.

19: And pursue the right course in thy going about and lower thy voice.
Surely the most hateful of voices is of braying asses.

King James Bible John Chapter 8 Verses 44-45

44: The father you spring from is the devil, and willingly you carry out his wishes.
He brought death to man from the beginning, and has never based himself on truth;
The truth is not in him. Lying speech is his native tongue; he is a liar and the father of lies.

45: But because I deal in the truth, you give me no credence.

Verses taken from Al-Quran and the King James Version of the Bible are included in these writings; not to promote or demonstrate any particular dogma (system of belief), devotion, religion, or spiritual viewpoints. These passages are incorporated for their commonsense observations, and their intellectual instructions.

It cannot be absolutely declared, without a doubt, that all the religiously-professed, divine instructions and perceived righteous messages, enclosed in every religiously-appointed spiritual text, are clearly the exact instructions from *The Most High.* Many are from the manipulative minds, the malevolently corrupt hearts, and iniquitous souls of those ruthless, calculating, scheming racists and chauvinists who manipulate, alter and manufacture fabricated adaptations of hallowed text, to persuade and control the hearts and minds of men. Divine volumes of understanding have been besmirched. Consequently, we must warily scrutinize heavenly scriptures with clear, logical thinking minds, to discover the obscured truths deviously concealed within their astonishingly enigmatic pages. If you control a person's God, you can control their thinking.

As new generations enter into each new epoch, every new generation ought to be more enlightened and more intellectually advanced than the preceding generations. However, upon examination, we learn that the most prevalent obstacles in their acquisitions of truth are the primordial, superstitious beliefs of those people who have long since passed. Many died because of their ignorant beliefs; as their falsities live on.

At this moment, this generation ought to be the most enlightened people in the history of this planet. Yet, examination once again reveals to us that the greatest dilemma facing our people today is our reluctance to face reality and to deal truthfully with that reality. A tremendous number of contradictory religions and troublesome religious beliefs are the single most prevailing obstacles blinding the majority of the people to the truth. Doctored doctrines do definitely devastate and divide dubiously dutiful and docile dullards.

We do recognize that, the vast majority of all humanity still remains illogically and *"faithfully"* locked within foundations of antediluvian beliefs, bizarre mythological philosophies, absurd primitive superstitions, and prehistoric doctrinaire religious beliefs. Centuries of erroneous teachings and continuous, contemporary indoctrinations daily fortify the detrimental racists' lies and disadvantageous religious beliefs; that trap us.

Too many people remain unbelievably spellbound by the myriad of chauvinistic lies, pseudo-superstitions, fabricated allegories and mythological fabrications of ancient, uninformed peoples. Too many still submit to conspicuous ignorance's of primitive peoples who existed eons before any contemporary technologies, and the proven scientific information, that we have come to know and master; ever even existed. In spite of all this, far too many people still believe in and fear the xenophobic racial fabrications, the stereotypical manipulations, and the patent lies and deceptions, which were designed to deceive, enslave and oppress the whole of humanity. Too many still submit to lies which are designed to subjugate and dominate them.

Al-Quran Surah 42 Ayat 170 - 171:

(170) When it is said to them, "Follow what Allah has revealed," the say: "Nay, we follow that wherein we found our fathers." What! Even though their fathers had no sense at all, nor did they follow the right way."

(171) And the parable of those who disbelieve is as the parable of one who calls out to that which hears no more than a call and a cry. Deaf, dumb, blind, so they have no sense.

Black people much too readily and willingly submit to, assimilate to, and gravitate to the vile and evil ways of the most oppressive, malevolent and murderous people to ever be acknowledged or engaged by them. Black people, for some peculiar reason unconditionally believe their vanquishers, and appear to love their tormenters; basking in their oppressive captivities as if they were some sort of wonderful rites of passage.

Black people have inadvertently, come to hate themselves, and mistrust themselves. Black people now thoughtlessly accept the disadvantageous, oppressive lies of their enslavers as their "Gospel, and Divine Truth!" They have deified their enemies and accepted as divine gospel, the obvious lies of their enemies.

The rational question that one must ask is, "Why?" Why would any group of people who have for so long, been so thoroughly and inhumanly victimized by another group of people now accept their victimizers, the fraudulence of their victimizers and the contemptible and immoral ways of their victimizers, as the truthful, appropriate, acceptable, and Godly way? What coherent explanation can Black people offer, for lifting up those viciously cruel, xenophobic peoples as their moral compass? Where is the sanity in this thinking?

How could that same group of victimized people who were so brutally enslaved and savagely persecuted by these racists, now commence to distinguish these same xenophobic persecutors as divine, noble, and righteous? Those same racists still hate Afrikans, ethnically mistreat Afrikans, disproportionately imprison Afrikans, steal from Afrikans, suppress Afrikans, devalue Afrikan lives, and routinely slaughter Afrikans so cruelly, callously and casually. Nonetheless, after all this viciousness, Black people still characterize their victimizers as the pinnacles of success, and lift up those same racist people to ordained positions; and as the personification of God Almighty! They worship graven images of their enemies as their God Almighty.

The disheartened and maltreated victims of the racists, instead of viewing the racists as incarnations, and manifestations of all things iniquitous, they instead begin to detest Afrikan characterizations, mentally and physically. When a people begin to internalize the self-loathing for themselves, and begin to worship their victimizers, even to the point of raising in effigy, their images, as the images of all things divine, to include God, and begin to bow down to those images, and worship those same racialist images as God Almighty; then those people have to be viewed, as a people who are suffering tremendously from the detrimentally disadvantageous affects of psychological damage. Those people have to be viewed as being insane.

Any logical or sane thinking people would view as detrimental, any images of any people who so pitilessly and mercilessly abducted them from their lands, removed their human characteristics dehumanizing them and selling their Afrikan bodies into chattel slavery; brutalizing them, raping, robbing, and murdering them so callously. To a sane thinking people, the racists would be acknowledged, as an enemy people and the devil incarnate; and not to be characterized, worshiped, or raised in effigy as the divine image of God.

Logical, lucid thinking people would demand that those most detrimental to Afrikans be seen as enemies. Any coherent peoples' thinking would demand that the racists be viewed as the embodiment of the most malevolent creatures ever known to them. Black peoples' devils should be depicted with white skin, and keen features. Unfortunately, devils, demons and iniquity are often depicted with Afrikan characteristics.

Afrikan people continue to survive, even after centuries of the most atrocious and horrendous episodes of racism, torture, enslavement, hatred and genocide to ever be committed against any people in the history of this planet. Despite incalculable endeavors to eradicate Afrikan people from this planet, we still exist.

The racialists have purposefully damaged Afrikans psychologically, spiritually and physically. They taught and teach Afrikans and the world that Afrikans were eternally damned and cursed Black, by a racist White God, and forever ordained to be slaves. They taught and teach Afrikans and the world that physically, the Afrikan's appearance is the most unattractive, and that the Caucasians' are the standard of beauty, which Afrikan people should cling to and aspire to as our standards of beauty, since Caucasians are the chosen people of God Almighty. Straighten your hair, lighten your skin and wear colored contacts to be beautiful.

Because of centuries of psychological damage Afrikans now abhor their own natural beauty; straightening their hair, lightening their skins, deforming themselves and killing themselves, trying to appear like, and to sound like, and to be like those very same people who should be to Afrikans; the most unattractive people on the face of this planet. We have been forever cursed by them; as we still worship the images of them.

This literary contribution is about truth. I beseech all who read this contribution, to open your minds, open your eyes, open your ears and unlock your hearts and souls. Examine these pages with open minds, and without prejudice. Objectivity and open-mindedness are keys to healing ourselves as a people. Before we can solve our problems we must first confess that we do have problems. Subsequently, we define our problems, make a diagnosis of our problems, and then we can prescribe and treat the symptoms; healing our physical, psychological and spiritual predicaments. Divine truth will restore Afrikans back to health.

Psychological, sociological, and spiritual damages are at the source of all our trials, and tribulations as an Afrikan people. Let us gain the knowledge, and examine the facts about, what we Afrikans have endured historically. Afrikans must commence to honestly acknowledge the enduring effects and the affects of the psychological scarring, that our experiences have left upon our Afrikan consciousnesses' as a people. It is an acknowledged and historically documented fact that Afrikan people were thoroughly and completely conquered, captured, devalued, dehumanized, and recreated to be "Negroes and niggers." Afrikans were deliberately physically abused, calculatedly psychologically maltreated and knowingly spiritually confused.

For these reasons, Afrikan peoples had to acquire the ability to become acclimated to whatever situations befell them. As Afrikan people, we have had to become very proficient at incorporating and enduring the racists' psychotically sadistic abuses, making them our norms on a regular basis. Afrikans had to learn to integrate the racists' iniquitously abusive behaviors, and those atrocities daily incurred, into their everyday lives. Their atrocities were made to become acceptable occurrences in our daily lives in desperate efforts to normalize, and make some sort of plausibly lucid justification, and understanding for Afrikans' suffering.

To endure as a people; rape, whipping, maiming, slavery, assaults, murders, and Afrikan dehumanization had become norms for Afrikans. In the process of learning to cope with, and accept as normal, their daily physical abuses, Afrikans became psychologically traumatized, physically brutalized, spiritually victimized and wholly eviscerated; allowing Afrikans to be absolutely re-created as chattel (the property of others).

As Afrikan people we continue to demonstrate unambiguous signs of psychological damage, continuously suffering psychotic episodes, and demonstrating detrimental and self-destructive behaviors, as a result of being sadistically and purposefully traumatized. Furthermore, as a result of psychological trauma it looks as if Afrikans have also developed a severe case of *Black Amnesia*. Many suffer selective forgetfulness.

Black Amnesia is a premeditated phenomenon designed to rob Afrikans of their historical foundations and their cultural identities. With no historical base and no cultural identity, we fall susceptible to re-creation.

Afrikans appear to suffer from unconscious, involuntarily, uncontrollable sessions of memory loss, which causes them to selectively fail to remember, misremember, or forget unbearably traumatic circumstances, situations and events. Afrikans have been deliberately and purposefully brainwashed, to the detriment of self, triggering tremendous amounts of psychologically damaging episodes. Afrikans were made to forget who they were, who they are, from whence they came, and from under what circumstances we arrived at this point of our existence. Many people now choose to be comfortably and blissfully ignorant amnesiacs.

When Afrikans did finally manage to escape the horrific nightmare of chattel slavery, many did not escape those plantations with their minds intact. Some say, "When the slaves left their plantations, many of them packed up, and left so hurriedly; during their haste in packing, many left their minds behind, as they forgot to pack them." When the Afrikan captives (our kidnapped fore parents), were finally unchained, they were set loose into an unsympathetic, racially xenophobic, hate-filled, culturally bigoted society, without benefit of psychological counsel or psychiatric support. No therapy or counseling after centuries of awful trauma.

We are talking about millions of foreign people who were thoroughly and completely brutalized, victimized and traumatized. Twenty-four hours a day, seven days a week, three hundred and sixty-five days a year. Can you even imagine; millions of traumatized, ignorant, uneducated Afrikans all of a sudden, evicted into the hostile streets of a country that found them to be abhorrent, despicable, and detestably evil creatures.

Just imagine; being constantly tortured 24 hours a day, seven days a week for 365 days a year. You are a sexually abused, physically abused, spiritually abused, and psychologically abused alien, released into a foreign land of iniquitous, uncompassionate people who have commanded you, and educated you to be inferior to them. Imagine being educated to think that you are hardly even a human being and in fact you are a bestial creation, created by the Devil, and cursed by almighty Caucasian God. Imagine, existing as a subhuman, so cursed that the public killing of you, was often sport and an act of entertainment for your racist oppressors. Imagine being loosed into a society with the understanding of being a cursed monster.

Afrikans were so thoroughly and completely dehumanized by their captors and their victimizers, that even the laws in the highest courts of this country did not differentiate Afrikans to be anything more than chattel (property), and judged them to be less than human. Afrikans were completely forced to absolutely forget their histories, required to remain utterly illiterate, and were legislated to completely relinquish any claims to their humanity. The highest courts in the land passed laws to remove their souls; making them chattel.

Damaged Afrikan psyches, due to physical and psychological traumas, creating a deeply detrimental and devastating sequence of psychoses has been determined to be the Afrikans' most considerable problem. The psychosomatic destructions perpetrated against Afrikans so many centuries in the past, continue on even today. Afrikans' original psychological afflictions have now evolved and are now manifest in various additional forms of injurious psychoses. Our psychoses have evolved, as everything in creation evolves. Our psychological trauma now manifests itself as apathetic behavior, low self-esteem, a warped sense of morality, self-abuse, self-hatred, fratricidal, misogynistic; and numerous other psychological disorders.

This discussion is about truth and our abilities to recognize deceptions, acknowledge realities, and accept all truths; no matter how inconvenient or how painful those truths may prove to be. When Afrikans began to accept and substitute the racists' fictitious beliefs, in lieu of established truths, Afrikans unquestionably began their descent into Caucasian created hells; which were created especially for the Afrikans' demise.

The racists concocted a multitude of racial fabrications, in correlation to race being the determining factor for human behavior, intelligence, and the propensity to prosper. We fell into their trap of racism, and the belief in the superiority of a particular race, because of race. Beliefs as to human abilities and capabilities being determined by race is a ridiculous and absolutely shameless racial lie. Racism is an unabashed lie.

As Afrikans, it is essential that we immediately begin to honestly and objectively acknowledge the truth of every circumstance in which we encounter. As people, we tend to get caught up in the "isms" game. We keep getting blissfully caught up in the oppressors' deception and many give the impression of reveling in their dishonesty. When Afrikans continue to ignorantly revel in those lies, and participate in those lies, the ill effects of longevity will always in the long run, sink its fangs into Afrikans; eventually transforming those racists' falsehoods into our Afrikan beliefs.

"If you can't convince them, confuse them!"

Former President Harry S. Truman

As Afrikan people, we have to learn to find the strength, the wisdom, and the courage to rise up out of set and dysfunctional modes of thinking. We have to find the ability to at least, listen to new ideas, with open minds and honest hearts. We have to discontinue; making prejudgments about new ideas and new ways of doing, or saying things. We must ascertain the wisdom, and the strength to unlearn many of the things we have been calculatingly conditioned (trained or eduKKKated), to unconsciously surrender to. Afrikans have to learn to genuinely listen to, and learn from all aspects and elements of the universe, with wisdom and knowledge; recognizing, understanding and knowing truth, and the factual characterization of reality.

Soon, the peoples' summit will once again be in session. Let us not continue to be distracted by religious discussions, or the foolish reverse racism discussions about magically endowed, ancient Black Egyptians, or the irresponsible discussions of racial superiority. I request each person reading this book, to suspend your beliefs, and truthfully research all logical ideas brought forward; for the next meeting with our people.

If there be any inaccuracies or fallacies discovered in any information, make them known, and continue to honestly search for those truths which will someday bring liberation to all. It is essential, that we continue our pursuit for the truth, the whole truth, and nothing but the truth; in our continuous pursuit of liberation!

"Theological Truth"

You claim your religion to be true; and no fallacy can be found in your theology,
Yet, we pointed out to you, evidences of astrology, and mythology, in your theology,
And we prove your so-called divine theology is little more than paganism and idolatry,
They dismissed as fallacies the evidences of astrology and mythology in your theology,
And, we've received no apologies upon revealing Greek mythology and Roman astrology,
As your theologies maintain the lies of pagans' ideologies in the hypocrisy of their theology!

"Mustafa Rasul Al-Amin"
(Sunday August 13, 2006)

"The Lies Of Liars"

Born in lies, born of lies, born full of lies, born because of lies them lives we live are lies!
Confused by lies, disillusioned by lies, consumed by lies, our realities are based on lies!
By closing our eyes to lies, we exist in lies, we tell lies, we live lies, and we become lies!
Preachers preach lies, teachers teach lies as parents tell, teach and live lives full of lies!
Our children learn lies, tell lies, and live those lies, as honesty and truth give way to lies!

Truth disguised is truth concealed, truth revised is truth unrevealed, truth denied; is a lie!

"Mustafa Rasul Al-Amin"
(102801)

"The Nigga Incantation"

As they chant, "nigga, nigga, nigga," they ignorantly internalize negativity,
Ignorantly believing that internalized negativities will increase niggas popularity,
Renamed niggas, and re-created niggas, by enemies which keep them in captivity,
Niggas now ignorantly believe; internalized negativities will increase niggas' prosperity,
As the descendants of Slaves ignorantly engage; in Caucasian celebrations of Afrikan slavery!

"Mustafa Rasul Al-Amin"
(Sunday May 28, 2006)

"The Greatest Liars"

(Mommy and Daddy; "Why have both of you been lying to me?")

People are always talking about how White men lie intentionally and repetitively,
And while it is an actual factual that White men do lie intentionally and repetitively,
They're still not the greatest liars that I ever did see, for the greatest liars lied to me,
And, the greatest liars that ever lied to me, happens to be, my Mommy, and my Daddy!

From birth, Mommy and Daddy have always told me and taught me emphatically,
That White men are habitual liars which Black people have to view as untrustworthy,
And, White men are historically known as the best liars, cheaters, and masters of thievery,
Forever stealing hopes, dreams, personalities, realities, countries, histories and even Afrikan me!

I sit here contemplating the things they've told and taught me, logically, and rationally,
For I have been educated to think for myself logically, rationally and of course honestly,
Confused by the contradictions of your words and deeds, which now seem illogical to me,
As you both tell me one thing and you do another, making me wonder if you've lied to me...

You tricked me into believing in the Demon called Santa Claus, and Christmas trees,
You tricked me into believing in the pagan goddess of Easter, complete with bunnies,
You tricked me into believing in the demons' rituals and Halloween for some candies,
You tricked me into believing in Jesus and Christian fallacies founded in mythologies!

As I examine his-story, mythology and the sciences of archeology and paleontology,
As I study psychology, sociology, ecology, biology, world theology, and trickenology,
My investigations of each of these entities tell me logically, rationally and objectively,
Mommy and Daddy, conclusively, and most assuredly, you've both been lying to me!

Now as I try to objectively, contemplate the depths of your deceptions and trickery,
After realizing that you have been lying to me and we exist in our oppressors' realities,
Conceivably, it would be logical for me, to view the two of you as instruments of my fatality,
Because we exist in oppressive realities of duality; as you allow our oppressors to control reality!

Mommy and Daddy, now that I have determined that you have been untruthful to me,
I must understand if your dishonesty with me was done to me intentionally or in sincerity,
Even if the lies you have been telling to me were perpetrated and perpetuated unintentionally,
The essential simple truth of the matter Mommy and Daddy is that you both; have been lying to me!

Lies are told arrogantly, openly, blatantly, knowingly, boldly, coldly, and intentionally,
Lies are told innocently, mistakenly, ignorantly, naively or completely unintentionally,
A lie is a lie no matter who it comes from, it is a lie when fallacies clash with realities,
Lies become more deceptive and destructive when lies are protected by our families!

People are always talking about how White men lie intentionally and repetitively,
And while it is an actual factual that White men do lie intentionally and repetitively,
They're still not the greatest liars that I ever did see, for the greatest liars lied to me,
And, the greatest liars that ever lied to me, happens to be, my Mommy, and my Daddy!

Mommy and Daddy; "Why have both of you been lying to me?"
Mommy and Daddy; "Why have both of you been lying to me?"
Mommy and Daddy; "Why have both of you been lying to me?"
Mommy and Daddy; "Why have both of you been lying to me?"

"Mustafa Rasul Al-Amin"
(101001)

"TRUTH LIBERATING"

If it is truth that binds

Why are there

So many lies - between

Lovers?

If truth is liberating

Why

Are people told

They look good when they don't

They are loved when they aren't

Everything is fine when it ain't

Glad you're back when you're not.

Black people in America

May not be made for the truth

We wrap our lives in disco

And Sunday morning sermons

While

Selling false dreams to our children

Lies

Are refundable

Can be bought on our revolutionary

Charge cards - As

We all catch the truth

On the next go round

If

It doesn't' hurt.

"Haki R. Madhubuti

"Fear Nothing But The Creator"

Gye Nyame

The enslavers and oppressors of Afrikan people fabricated a plethora of race based falsities pertaining to race being the determining factor for human behavior and intelligence; and the world slipped into the trap of racism, and the convictions of the superiority of a particular race, because of their race. The belief that human abilities and capabilities are determined by race is an absurd and barefaced, xenophobic lie.

They say that, "It's hard to teach old dogs new tricks." As we become Afrikan elders, we older folks must discover the strength, the wisdom and the courage to come up out of our set modes of thinking. We must discover the ability to at least listen to new ideas, with objective minds and sincere hearts. We must stop being so condemnatory about new ideas and new ways of doing, or thinking about, or even saying things. We must find the ability to discover the wisdom and the strength to unlearn many of the things have been forcefully instilled into us. True elders patiently listen to all ideas with wisdom, objectivity, and sincerity.

Shortly, our peoples' meetings will recommence. Let us begin again with truth on our agendas. I implore every person reading these pages to temporarily suspend your beliefs and research all reasonable ideas, thoughts and suggestions brought forward within these pages. If there be errors or fallacy found in these pages, make them known, and continue to search for the truth, that will someday set everyone free. It is imperative that we continue our search for the truth, the whole truth and nothing but the truth, as sincere endeavors to liberate the minds of humanity!

If there be errors of falsities found within the pages of this book, please bring them to my attention, and to the attention of our people, and please accept my humblest apologies; for it is not my intention mislead or misinform anyone, any longer, for any reason. My goal is to teach, inform and liberate misinformed minds from the tyranny of deception.

"Go Back And Reclaim Our Past"

"Sankofa"

(Chapter Two)

"Niggerology"

Niggerology - 1 a: the branch of knowledge concerning the creation, examination, study, research, affects and effect of phenomenon known as nigger(s)

b: The laws and phenomenon relating to the word nigger, or to the human reconstruction and transformation of people into nigger(s)

2 a: the science concerning the study of the nigger(s) psychiatry, psychology, sociology and the behaviors in relation to a particular field of knowledge or activity.

b; regarding, about, concerning in relation to or pertaining to nigger(s)

3. The Willie Lynch curriculum (methods/tactics)

"Niggerology 101," is an earnest endeavor to both illustrate and define both the phenomenon of the word nigger, and the human personality called nigger. It is a sincere attempt to demonstrate to Afrikan people and the world, the calamitous consequences of giving your blessings to others, as they undertake efforts to modify your name, change your characteristics, and restructure you and your history. When we know that others are mean spirited, xenophobic racialists who do not have Afrikans' best interests at heart; we must simultaneously, question their agendas and challenge their authority. Nigger is an immoral creation concocted for the benefit of our oppressors and to the disadvantage of Afrikans. There is no other single word possessing more evil and more power than the demonic, despicable, and iniquitous word; nigger!

Completely understanding that the word nigger is in reality a "terminological" statement of detriment; and completely understanding that when the word was fashioned, it was rudimentarily utilized scientifically as a descriptive, by behavioral specialists, in conjunction with scientific hypotheses premeditated to describe a people's habits, cultural backgrounds, and psychological, and physiological structures; this proves that the nigger, in its assignment, in correlation to Afrikan people, is more than just a simple word.

Wholly understanding that the intolerant racists had designed, fashioned, and produced a fully functional, economically profitable, commercial enterprise (the slave trade industry), which included the utilization of behavior specialists implementing behavioral sciences; this makes it necessary for us to understand that the racists had (have) a branch of knowledge dedicated to the study and the examination of niggers, and nigger behaviors which kept (keeps) their industry so very profitable and so very efficient, for so very long.

Completely understanding that rudimentary sciences were being implemented from the original capture of the slaves (how to and where to efficiently capture the most slaves), to transportation of the slaves (loose pack, tight pack), to institutional control of slaves (The Willie Lynch Theory), we must begin to understand that there were and still are; departments and branches of science committed to the controlling of niggers.

So, completely understanding that there is a "branch of knowledge (a science)" dedicated to the study of niggers, the next logical step to bringing this branch of knowledge out of the shadows of secrecy and into the light of awareness is to give it a name. When we can name it we can recognize it. So, from this time forward, "Niggerology" shall now be the name of the branch of knowledge which studies all aspects of the terminological word nigger, to include the study of the affects and effects of this iniquitous creation.

Completely understanding the terminological expressions and intents of the word nigger, and the mindset of those racists responsible for implementing this damnable word of wickedness, is an absolute necessity. We must understand that we can never afford to miscalculate the racists, in their thinking, or in their logic. It is for these reasons that we ***cannot***, claim responsibility for the creation or the origination of this branch of knowledge. Based upon factual logic, our knowledge of the racists, and our extensive comprehension of the mindsets of those racists; our observations logically dictate, this branch of knowledge is undeniably already in existence. We know that the racists studied Afrikans, and we know that the racists, in spite of everything, to this day, they are still both studying and experimenting on Afrikans.

So, logically thinking:

(1) If the racists have studied and are still studying Afrikans;
(2) If the racists' agendas are to transform Afrikans into niggers and;
(3) If the racists refer to Afrikans as the niggers that they perceive us to be;

Since we know that the suffix ***-ology*** is defined as, ***the study of,*** and since we now know, that the racists renamed the Afrikans they study ***niggers;*** then realistically ***the study of niggers*** should be articulated as *"Niggerology."* When most people study things, they study them with a purpose. Controlling people study things for the purposes of manipulating, re-creating, and controlling those things in which they study.

I'll wager you that deep inside the vast caverns of their top-secret laboratories and contained in the many pages of their classified documents, they coined the phrase, *"Niggerology."* It's only logical. Therefore, I will not erroneously make the claim of discovering or creating this branch of scientific knowledge. I won't even make the claim of coining the phrase, *"Niggerology,"* for I truthfully believe, this term already stands in existence. My claims are those of revelation, illumination, and clarification, regarding the existence of the word and the substantiation of the racists' manipulative programs of oppression and re-creation.

Whether Willie Lynch existed or not, this narrative is a demonstration of the realities, and of the existence of the science we now call Niggerology. In the Willie Lynch narrative, William Lynch in 1712 gave a very comprehensive and detailed speech to a group of slave owners, instructing them on how to manage their slaves mentally, physically and spiritually. His knowledge was complete and thorough, and provides clear evidence of a meticulously intricate and time consuming type of scientific research. He knew the Afrikans psychologically, physiologically and theologically, and this permitted him to calculate and evaluate Afrikan reactions to particular mental, physical and spiritual stimuli. Willie Lynch was a behavioral scientist.

We all know what is happening and what has happened. The objective of this book is to reveal truths and to stimulate awareness. The purpose of this book is to uncover untruths and to divulge falsehoods. If we bring to light and make plain the many falsehoods that ***lie*** right before our very eyes, hiding in plain sight; we simultaneously initiate our process of liberation. Racial antagonists have taken the descriptive nigger and transformed it into a word which intentionally denigrates, dehumanizes, and destroys Afrikan people mentally, physically and spiritually. The term nigger is an acknowledgment of submission to re-creation.

Never underestimate the racists and understand that creation of nigger is not an inadvertent phenomenon of happenstance. The word nigger is premeditated, and fashioned with a purpose. The word nigger was fashioned to remove the human characteristic from Afrikans. The word nigger was produced to reclassify Afrikans outside of the human race and to place them in bestial, animalistic, non-human, and sub-human classifications and categories. Submission to the word nigger acknowledges completion of re-creation.

As logical thinkers, we must understand there is a process called *Niggerization.* Niggerization is a wicked process within Niggerology. Niggerization is to be utilized as an adjective which is a demonstration of the actual procedure for constructing niggers. Niggerization is a process, resulting from diligently widespread programs of immorally fraudulent, pseudo-scientific research, which we have now called, *"Niggerology."*

Successes of this process are evidenced by the extensive and ongoing research of Afrikans' sociological, psychological, physiological and theological characteristics, which are occurring, even at this moment.

The slave traders created and developed the science, of Niggerology to better develop more manageable and *unconstructive* niggers, which are now unleashed on Black communities and Afrikan people. Niggers are to be compared to a type of biological weapon to be controlled and used by racial extremists, for their benefit. Niggers are biological weapons, methodically designed, to keep Black communities and Afrikans subordinate, and submissively attached to the racists. The racists fashioned this weapon to support them in their genocidal programs, which target Afrikans for population control, and reinforces White supremacy.

The racists create teachable nigger behaviors and counterfeit nigger cultures, to contribute to the general overall devastation of Afrikans. Disadvantageous programs of nigger indoctrinations and spurious rites of passage are daily launched against the Afrikans' psyche. Beginning at birth, the racists keep in check the minds, bodies and souls of Afrikans. From the cradle to the grave, Afrikans are "eduKKKated" to become niggers and to be inferior to every other race of people on the face of this planet and then; the victims are blamed for their own deplorable conditions. Deplorable conditions which are premeditatedly initiated and instigated by the racists for the subjugation, manipulation, incarceration and destruction of Afrikan people.

The best that Afrikans can hope to accomplish in the racists' social order is a type of pseudo-equality, via assimilation. Equality through the eyes of the racists means to surrender our characterizations, customs, cultural accomplishments, and even surrender our very souls to them. Afrikan people must be passionate about becoming completely absorbed into Caucasians' psyches. To be AmeriKKKan is to be assimilated.

AmeriKKKa is not a melding pot, which blends the cultures of all those existing within her boundaries and borders. In reality, AmeriKKKa is a cauldron of assimilation, where all who enter have to assimilate to the customs and whims of the dominant culture. Afrikans must not only be agreeable to become Caucasian in thought and in mannerisms; in the Afrikans' assimilations, the Afrikans have to include an enthusiasm, for a physical transformation and assimilation. That's why we so many Black are people craving straight hair, colored eyes and light skin, and yearn so desperately for thin noses and "*deceivingly*" thin lips.

Recognizing and understanding the branch of knowledge now identified as Niggerology, and the process of Niggerization, is crucial for the development and liberation of Afrikan people. In most instances, when rational thinking people know what is happening to them, they begin to rectify all situations which proved to be detrimental to them. The first step to solving a problem is to recognize the problem and identify the problem by name. We have defined the problem, and called it by name. Now it is time for us to begin to solve the problem of niggas, niggers, niggerization and the iniquitous theology of Niggerology!

Niggerology (*An alternate and more in depth definition of the body of knowledge; and science of niggers)*

1. a: The secret, racially motivated division of science that pertains to the creation of, the examination of, the experimentation of, the manipulation of, the influences on and the influencing of, and the end results of the word nigger; the man-made being called nigger, and the psychological nigger behaviors inculcated into people of Afrikan descent, for the purposes of evolutionary (devolutionary) manipulation.

b: The laws and phenomenon relating to the psychological and physical creation, and manipulation of niggers as individuals and as a group.

c: The physical, psychological and theological study of re-creating Afrikans; for the intents of constructing niggers, nigger mentalities and behaviors in correlation to a particular field of study, knowledge or activity.

d: The science concerning niggers.

2. The creation, examination, manipulation and study of niggers a.k.a. niggas.

3. The Willie Lynch curriculum (The Willie Lynch training methods and tactics)

"Mustafa Rasul Al-Amin"
(Resubmitted Wednesday November 25, 2009)

(Chapter Three)

"NIGGER"

Niggers are scared of revolution,
But niggers shouldn't be scared of revolution,
Because revolution is nothing but change,
And all niggers do is change.

Niggers come in from work and change into pimping clothes,
To hit the street and make some quick change.
Niggers change their hair from black to red to blonde,
And hope like hell their looks will change.
Niggers kill others just because one didn't receive the correct change.
Niggers change from men to women, from women to men,
Niggers change, change, change!
You hear Niggers saying, "Things are changing!"
Things are changing, yeah things are changing.
Nigger things into Black Nigger things!
Black Nigger things that go through all kinds of changes,
They change in the day; they make demands and rave, "Black Power, Black Power!"
And the change that comes at night when they sigh alone.....
Light thighs, woo; light thighs!
Niggers always going through bullshit changes,
But when it comes for a real change,
Niggers are scared of revolution.

Niggers are actors, Niggers are actors.....
They act like they're in a hurry to get the put backs of the great white hope.
Niggers ought to act like Malcolm,
And when the white man doesn't react towards him like he did Malcolm,
Niggers want to act violently!
Niggers want to act a fool.....
And trip causing white people to say,
"What makes you act like that?"
Niggers act like you ain't never seen act before,
But when it comes to acting out revolution Niggers say,
"I can't dig that action!"
Niggers are scared of revolution.

Niggers are very un-together people.
Niggers talk about getting high and riding round in Ells,
Niggers should get drunk and ride to hell!
Niggers talk about pimping, pimping that what was yours pimping mines.
Just to be pimping is a hell of a line.

Niggers are players! Niggers are players! Niggers are players!
Niggers play football, basketball and baseball,
White the white man is cutting off their balls.
Niggers tell you that they are ready to go out and be liberated,
But when you say let's go take our liberation,
Niggers reply, "I was just playing!"
Niggers are playing with revolution, illusion.
Niggers are scared of revolution.

Niggers fuck! Niggers Fuck! Niggers Fuck!
Niggers fuck, fuck.
Niggers love the word fuck.
They think they're fucking cute.
They fuck you around.
The first thing they say when they're mad is "fuck it."
You play a little too much with them they say "fuck you."
Try to be nice to them they fuck you over.
When it's time to TCB niggers are somewhere fucking.
Niggers don't realize while they're doing all this fucking they're getting fucked around.
But when they do realize it's too late, so all niggers do is just get fucked . . . up!
Niggers talk about fucking...
Fucking that... Fucking this...
Fucking yours... Fucking my sis,
Not knowing what they fucking for,
Ain't fucking for love and appreciation,
Just fucking to be fucking,

Niggers fuck white thighs, brown thighs, yellow thighs.
Niggers fuck ankles when they run out of thighs.
Niggers fuck Sally Linda and Sue.
And if you don't watch out niggers will fuck you...
Niggers would fuck; fuck if fuck could be fucked.
But when it comes to fucking for revolutionary causes...
Niggers say, “FUCK Revolution!
Niggers are scared of revolution.

Niggers love to hear Malcolm speak,
But they didn’t love Malcolm.
Niggers love everything but themselves,
But I am a lover too! Yes I am a love too!
I love Niggers! I love Niggers! I love Niggers!
Because, Niggers are me, and I love that which is me.
I love to see Niggers go through changes!
I love to see Niggers act!
Love to see Niggers make them plays and shoot the shit!

But;
There is one thing about Niggers.....
I do not love.....

“Niggers Are Scared Of Revolution!”

The Last Poets-1970

The Last Poets are right! Niggers are scared of revolution!

Nigger – 1) NEGRO - usu. taken to be offensive
2) A member of any dark-skinned race –
Usu. taken to be offensive

Webster's New Collegiate Dictionary

Nigger! Nigger is a very powerful word. It is quite possible that this harmful racial malediction is perhaps one of the most powerful words to ever be spoken in contemporary language. This wicked six letter word does possess more destructive negativity, than any other word of the enormously abundant languages of the planet. The word nigger, is so much more powerful than any other racial, ethnic, religious, sexual, or culturally charged, vulgarly offensive epithets and profanities, which appear to be materializing, with ever more frequency. Each day, this vulgarity is utilized more and more regularly. Its daily usage is becoming more common, and seems to be entering into our conversations with even more of a sense of normalcy in our daily personal exchanges, as well as in those public environments of the internet, media print, and the radio and television airwaves. Its usage on *The Cartoon Channel* doesn't even warrant an eyebrow raise.

The word nigger is a denigrating and dehumanizing racial characterization that is utilized in most English speaking or White dominated countries. These countries include the United States, the United Kingdom, Canada, Sweden, Australia, Austria, France, Germany, South Africa, Japan, Israel, China, Korea, Russia and the former countries of the Soviet Union. In these, and in so many other countries all over the world, time and time again, this profanity nigger is consistently carried forward, and placed front and center, as an offensively demeaning, bigoted, racial reference maliciously directed towards every person of Afrikan descent, with a venomously toxic, xenophobic-based, racial and cultural hatred.

Thoughtlessly, and most assuredly very dangerously, too many people are beginning to surrender to the irrational concept that, *"Words only have the power that we bestow upon them."* Yet, I say unto you that, this one word, this curse word, this iniquitous incantation, with its six letters, and two syllables, is powerful enough to completely annihilate, eradicate, exterminate and obliterate an entire race of people. The word "nigger" is just that powerful!

The Etymology Of The Word Nigger

It is so very necessary that we learn and understand the etymology or study of words' histories and their origins, for us to ascertain a straightforward understanding of the real definitions of words. Nigger is the most historically offensive word of the world's speech. It is so very important for us to know with certainty where this word comes from. We must learn its genesis, and its history to fully understand, comprehend, and be acquainted with its meaning to fully appreciate the pejorative power of this evil racial dysfunction.

To truly understand and appreciate the incredible power of this iniquitous word, one must first understand the etymology or the origins and the actual world history of the word. It is so very important that everyone be made conscious as to how and why this contemptible word was created. All must understand how this word was intended to be used, and how the word is actually used. When everybody begins to completely realize that the intent of this word was to dehumanize, redefine, humiliate and to re-create in their entirety, the whole of Afrikan people; perhaps then people will begin to understand both the destructive, genocidal intent of this word and the maliciously devastating power of this word. Clarification provides illumination.

This six letter word, nigger, dates back to the late sixteenth century. However, the contemporary spelling of this word did not actually appear until approximately two hundred years later. Nigger is fundamentally a derivative of the French descriptive nègre, which is a derivative of the Dutch and Germans' adjectives neger, of which, all are derivatives of the Latin descriptive Niger, and Later the Spanish adjective Negro.

Initially, every interpretation of the word nigger was by definition, an adjective, which described the color black. Assigning this adjective to Afrikans as a racial and personality designation would become the first step in the process of alienating Afrikans from their lands and from the roles of human beings. Removing peoples' racial and cultural identities and replacing them with an abstract adjective has proved effective.

In America, Niger would transmute into neger, neggar and later transformed into nigger. So at the outset, we discover that nigger was nothing more than a Latin adjective which basically describes the color black.

The word neger, which was sometimes spelled neggar, flourished in a number of northern sections, of the United States. Common utilization of the word was very widespread, in numerous provinces for example; In New York under the Dutch, the Moravian communities of Philadelphia, and many of the Pennsylvanian Dutch and German communities. Offered as clear evidence of these facts are the *African Burial Grounds* in New York City. *The African Burial Grounds* were originally called *"Begraaf Plaats van de Neger."*

The earliest acknowledged discovery of the modern spelling of nigger is from 1786, in poet Robert Burns' poem, *"The Ordination."* However, *"The Random House Historical Dictionary of Slang,"* declares that the spelling "nigger" is in reality an editorial inaccuracy, and Burns' original manuscript uses the original word, *"Niger."* This antiquated spelling of the word Niger dates to the year 1574. Always keep in mind; niger is the Latin adjective of the color black, and Niger and Negro share a common derivation.

Below is a passage from Robert Burns' 1786 poem, *"The Ordination":*

Come, let a proper text be read,
An' touch it aff wi' vigour,
How graceless Ham laugh at his dad,
Which made Canaan a ***nigger****;*
Or Phineas drove the murdering blade,
Wi' whore-abhorring rigour;
Or Zipporah, the scauldin jad,
Was like a bluidy tiger,
I' th' inn that day.

Nigger As A Casual And Common Descriptive

Historians passionately argue the point that, during the time when the abomination of chattel slavery was instigated and tolerated in America, and for several decades thereafter, the word nigger was an ordinary, common, casually used term for Afrikan people. Originally, the word nigger (on its surface) was intended to be an adjective, a descriptive phrase which depicted all *"dark skin"* people of Afrikan descent.

Historians forcefully argue that it was later that the word eventually became associated with presumptions of "inherent inferiority." Coupled with the racist, stereotypical characterizations of the ethnicity, which the word denotes, nigger has grown into a powerful racial malediction utilized to abuse, demean, debase, and dehumanize all dark-skin peoples of Afrikan ancestry. Pejoratively speaking, there is not a meaner word.

Nearly every historians concedes; early in America's history the word nigger was not originally considered to be disparaging or hateful by the enslavers of Afrikan People. Nigger was only a descriptive denotative. They assert as an example of the word's common usage, Mark Twain's usage of the word in *"Huckleberry Finn."* By the standards of his day, he is not necessarily being intentionally offensive although, even then the word nigger would not be utilized in refined society. Mark Twain's usage of the term was as a marker used to characterize and illustrate the racial, social and economic status of the storybook characters who commonly uttered this racially injurious word. Nigger wasn't offensive to contemporary Caucasian users.

To additionally illustrate the casualness, and the common usage of the word; in a 1700 quote by Judge Samuel Seawall, he uses the word in one of his denunciations of slavery:

Excerpt from the 1700 pamphlet: *"The Selling of Joseph" (Printed in 1700*

> *And yet 'tis to be feared, we have no other kind of title to our Niggers. Therefore all things whatsoever ye would that men should do to you, do ye even so to them: for this is the Law and the Prophets.*

Gradually, sociable discourse increasingly used the term Negro, which dates to at least 1555, and nigger, became relegated to the vulgar tongue. The consistently increasing offensiveness of the word gradually grew more offensive over time, especially in the 20th century. By the 20th century, the word nigger had developed into, and become one of the most extremely offensive and racially explosive terminologies to ever be uttered. Nigger at one time was pretty much the only taboo word in Americans' conversations.

Among Caucasians the word is still taboo but, in some bizarre twist of logic, many people find it strangely interesting that the only acceptable use of the word nigger is when African-Americans utilize it to refer to themselves. Do illogical attempts at reclamation make this word less offensive or less destructive?

There are much similar reclamations; like the words queer and fag among homosexuals. These are weak attempts to rob a word, of the offensiveness of the word. Far too many foolishly try to exploit these vulgar words amongst themselves to *"affectionately"* refer to themselves. Investigations has additionally brought to light, that even when people of other races verbally assault one another; increasingly the harshest form of verbal shame that they can offer-up, is to call the other a nigger, or suggest they acting like a nigger.

In early American literature we often witness numerous instances of the utilization of the word nigger, with *"seemingly"* no intended pessimistic connotations. Their judgment of the word nigger as derogatory is no doubt related to the fact that, the Afrikan race itself was widely regarded as inferior by those of Caucasoid races. The *"coerced lessons"* of self-hatred, imposed by the dominant cultures, upon all people of Afrikan descent dictates that we also view ourselves to be inferior, to all other races of this planet's people.

Although it was said that the word was not meant to be offensive its naissance, history still bears witness to the fact, that this iniquitous word "nigger," was calculatingly and purposefully designated for dark-skin Afrikan peoples, in scheming undertakings, to diminish and eventually appropriate their humanity. Afrikan people were purposefully and by design reduced to a non-human descriptive term, a color, in attempts to disassociate them from any history, humanity and historical land mass. This was perpetrated to complete the wicked process, of making Afrikan people, be a bestial people. A people with no identity, no past, no history, no future and no humanity of their own! They were SLAVE: Stolen, Lost And Viciously Educated.

Deuteronomy 28:32 Thy sons and daughter shall be given unto another people, and thine eyes shall look, and fail with longing for them all the day long: and there shall be no might in thy hand.

Deuteronomy 28:64 And the Lord shall scatter thee among all people, from one end of the earth even unto the other; and there thou shalt serve other gods, which neither thou nor thy fathers have known, even wood and stone.

The factual etymology of the word nigger bears witness to the fact, that from the first time it was utilized to descriptively designate people of Afrikan ancestry, the underlying reasons of the racial designation was to steal the souls of Afrikan people and rob them of their humanity. It was the aim of the racists to transform a passionate people into an inanimate, soulless non-human entity; to be bought, sold and exploited to the detriment of Afrikans, and for the strengthening of White supremacy.

By reducing a people to a color and into an inhuman object, you rob them of their humanity, and allow for their captivity. When you let others reduce you to a color, when you let others turn you into a thing, when you let others define you, claim you and name you; you in turn, become robbed of your humanity, and are portrayed by your captors, as their chattel (property), and you become the bestial captives of the world!

Nigger comes from the Latin root for black. The word was used in both England and America around the 17th century. Around 1825, abolitionists and blacks began feeling the word was hurtful to them. After the Civil War, the word "nigger" became the most commonly used term to describe the blacks. Even though the word was at first not meant to offend, such powerful white men as George Conrad continually used it during public speaking and argued that the word was not meant to be offensive.

The Random House Historical Dictionary of American Slang

Nigger: The obsolete spelling "Niger" dates back to 1574 derived from the Latin word meaning "black"

Stereotypical Niggers

The Racists Don't Even Have Compassion For Our Children

Nigger is the racists' descriptive for dark-skin people Afrikan ancestry and has constantly been associated with the presumption of inherent racial inferiority, inferior intelligence, deceitfulness, depravity, criminality, sexual promiscuity, buffoonery and social backwardness.

"Mustafa Rasul Al-Amin"

"The Nigga Incantation"

As they chant, "nigga, nigga, nigga," they ignorantly internalize negativity,
Ignorantly believing that internalized negativities will increase niggas popularity,
Renamed niggas, and re-created niggas, by enemies which keep them in captivity,
Niggas now ignorantly believe; internalized negativities will increase niggas' prosperity,
As the descendants of Slaves ignorantly engage; in Caucasian celebrations of Afrikan slavery!

"Mustafa Rasul Al-Amin"
(Sunday May 28, 2006)

"Understand"

You must understand the knowledge and truth of things seemingly unperceived,
I'm trying to make you perceive the truth, by insuring the information is received,
Understanding truth will protect you from those purposely keeping you deceived

Do you understand the words that are coming out of my mouth?
Do you understand the words from my mouth are from my soul?

"Mustafa Rasul Al-Amin"
(Sunday June 10, 2007)

"DYSFUNCTIONAL SOCIALIZATION"
(Socialized To The Detriment Of Ourselves)

We're being socialized to the detriment of ourselves,
Tele-hypnotized to despise the splendor of ourselves,
Socialized dysfunctional to normalize the hating ourselves,
And psycho-sociologically programmed to destroy ourselves!

Dysfunctional Socialization is when abnormality becomes a logical act of normalization,
And is an act of intentionally introducing dysfunctional behavior as normal socialization,
To entire generations of non-Caucasians simply for the reasons of racial discrimination,
As a steadfast remedy, for the racial insecurities, of those of the Caucasian persuasion!

No matter to the Caucasian that the hue of a nation is Afrikan, Arabic, Haitian or Asian,
When appropriated by way of Caucasian colonization, no matter the hue of the population,
Caucasian colonization, is their sole rationalization, and the foundation for racial justification,
And, Caucasian domination, is their rationalization and is their foundation for ethnic purification,
Whilst Caucasians dole out those racially dysfunctional normalizations for all "Hue-man" populations!

Upon thorough examination we find the media is controlling Caucasian nations,
And distort, destroy and discard all positive exemplifications, and demonstrations,
Of any and all "Hue-man" examples of racial achievements with no indemnifications,
Which means; never any type of compensation for the detrimental racial modifications!

Hocus pocus the joke's on us as we are constantly urged to use our imagination,
When the reality of the situation is racial modification through media-prestidigitation,
Breeding Dysfunctional Socialization, not simply for the purposes of racial gratification,
For the historical substantiation of racial colonization also substantiates racial gentrification!

Dysfunctional Socialization is when as we flip the TV stations from station to station,
While TV stations display detrimental, stereotypical images of us to the world's nations,
AmeriKKKa's re-creation of a people's naturalization is based solely upon criminalization,
AmeriKKKa's re-creation of a people's foundation is of sexual depravations and inebriation!

Dysfunctional Socialization disguised by the creation of media induced prestidigitation,
Have created cultural stipulations for the perpetuation of prohibited economic situations,
Where cocaine becomes a culturally economic situation with the slightest of modifications,
And it's insane when cocaine and crime becomes a feasible source of economic stimulation!

Socialized dysfunctional to accept as normal; Afrikan generations of a thug nation!
Socialized dysfunctional to accept as normal; generations of Afrikan incarceration!
Socialized dysfunctional to accept as normal; Afrikan depravation, and inebriation!
Socialized dysfunctional to accept as normal; Afrikans being niggers in this nation!

Socialized dysfunctional per racial modification, via media-prestidigitation;

We're being socialized to the detriment of ourselves,
Tele-hypnotized to despise the splendor of ourselves,
Socialized dysfunctional to normalize the hating ourselves,
And psycho-sociologically programmed to destroy ourselves!

"Mustafa Rasul Al-Amin"
(082201)

(Chapter Four)

"NIGGA"
(Identity Crisis)

Never Ignorant Getting Goals
Accomplished N.I.G.G.A.

Tupac Shakur

Nigger, darky, Negro, and colored; at various times all were acceptable adjectives when it pertains to the descriptions of people of Afrikan ancestry. Each descriptive is now thought to be either racially offensive or contemptible racial slurs. Each descriptive was assigned to Afrikan people by those which hated them the most, and each descriptive is reflective of the racists' intentions to rob Afrikans of their identities, their histories, their lands and the characterizations which make Afrikans be Afrikans. Now nigga springs forth.

Since the 1980s, one widespread argument amongst many Afrikan people in America, centers around the enunciations, pronunciations, intonations, and definitions the words nigger and nigga. Many contend that nigga and nigger are two altogether dissimilar words and some make the argument that nigga is basically nigger pronounced phonetically; and is nothing more than tonal expressions of Afrikan-American dialects. However, many argue that nigga is synonymous with acknowledged slang words such as dude, man, guy or partner. Many also contend that, when Afrikan-Americans utilize nigga, it is used to express kinship or affection i.e. "What's up my nigga? It is also used to express anger and hatred. "Fuck you; Nigga!"

Advocates of this neo-revisionist use of the term believe nigga in its vernacular pronunciation is harmless. On the other hand, many presume it draws the line between Black people who are victims of racism, and Black people who are empowered as fashionable, accepted, hip, street-smart individuals. In an interview, Tupac Shakur explains, *"Niggers was the ones on the rope, hanging off the thing; Niggas is the ones with gold ropes, hanging out at clubs."* As if wearing gold ropes, hanging out at clubs are fruitful endeavors.

Ah, the ignorance of youth and the frailty of the elders for not rectifying them.......

Opponents of this view argue that nigga is nothing more nigger, enunciated with a cultural dialect, and the revisionists' spelling is merely a phonetic representation of the word, as it always has been pronounced in Afrikan-American and southern dialects, and nothing more. It must always be kept in mind that, Nigger is commonly pronounced as nigga, by many who use it in anger, and intend it to be an offensive racial slur.

While proponents of the neo-revisionist usage of nigga contend they have reclaimed the word and robbed it of its racist connotations. I absolutely dispute this. I maintain that the revisionists' use has not changed the word's centuries-old, racist nature. The words are synonymous and they comprise the same historical definition. Most dark-skin peoples of the world still consider this bigoted idiom offensive and inappropriate in all contexts. Nigger is in no way acceptable in any context when used by non-Afrikans. So, why should it be acceptable to the very people who are moment to moment victimized by its usage? This profanity's usage by members of any other ethnic groups are always condemned and viewed as racist, but usage by those within the victims' group is oftentimes celebrated and commonly overlooked.

The enlightening passage below, from the *"African American Registry,"* echoes this sentiment:

> *Neo-revisionist arguments for the use of "nigga" may not be true to life. Brother (Brotha) and Sister (Sistah) are terms of endearment. Nigger was always and still is a word of disrespect. The artificial dichotomy between Blacks or African-Americans (respectable and middle-class) and niggers (disrespectable and lower class) ought to be challenged.*

Blacks, from slavery 'til today, have internalized many negative images that white society cultivated and broadcast about black skin and black people. This is mirrored in cycles of self- and same-race hatred. The use of the word nigger by blacks reflects this hatred, even when the user is unaware of the psychological forces involved. Nigger is the ultimate expression of white racism and white superiority no matter how it is pronounced.

Sociologists commonly point to Black-on-Black violence and its association with gangsta rap-- the phenomenon most responsible for the rise in the revisionist use of the term among some Black youth -- as a manifestation of the self-destructive, self-loathing mind-set referred to above.

There is also a marked class difference in African-American use of the term. The more highly educated, the higher one's socioeconomic status, regardless of age, the less likely one is to use the term self-referentially, if at all.

Finally, if continued use of the word lessened its damage, then nigger would not hurt or cause pain now.

"The African American Registry"

Continuously, many endeavor to reclaim this profanity with weak attempts to rob this despicable vulgarity of its offensiveness. Frequently, thoughtlessly, and destructively, far too many people attempt to develop this iniquitously blasphemous invocation as a term of endearment amongst themselves, in faulty attempts to affectionately refer to one another. Knowing the historical legacy of the word, when will we ever gather the strength, courage and maturity to eradicate this iniquitous word from our vocabularies, in conjunction with the vocabularies of all others? When will Afrikans begin to be adamant in demanding that ***"we"*** stop referring to ourselves as niggers and niggas, just as we (on the surface), don't allow those of other races, to refer to Afrikans as niggers or niggas?

At this present moment in time, many Afrikan-Americans thoughtlessly endeavor to appropriate the curse, nigger, and they continuously, erroneously, and illogically attempt to resurrect one of the most derogatory and destructive terminologies to ever be created and make it into a self-referential term. Ignorantly and to the detriment of Afrikans, many commonly endeavor to utilize this despicable term as a term of familiarity, endearment and even kinship; as it both destroys and robs all Afrikan people of all their power.

The Evolution of Afrikan Identities

Since arriving in America, Afrikan people have unquestionably undergone devastating identity crises, and overwhelming psychological personality disorders. Since even before the first abductees embarked upon those damned slave ships; Afrikan identities and personalities were already being stolen and manipulated to the detriment of all Afrikans. Once Afrikans disembarked those devilish ships they were not allowed to remember or to even talk about Afrika, freedom or memories of their pasts. Afrikans were made to forget who they were and from whence they came. The racists made it unlawful for Afrikans to even remember!

This premeditated theft of identity, personality and humanity was a calculated act to more securely exploit a people for all their knowledge, rob a people of all wealth and to enslave that people to acquire free labor and expertise. The theft of identity, personality and humanity allows the enslavers to create, recreate and control the cultures, identities, personalities, and the degrees of humanity; to be allowed for the enslaved.

First they created for Afrikans; realities based upon a slave culture, which gave Afrikans bigoted Christian religions which taught them that their conditions were the result of an angry White God cursing them into slavery. The racists took away their religions, histories, cultures and Gods, and replaced them with things most beneficial to White supremacy. They changed the Afrikans' diets, renamed them nigger, and seized all freedoms; including the freedom of thought. When you control a man's thoughts, you control the man.

"Nigger is the ultimate expression of white racism and white superiority no matter how it is pronounced."

"The African American Registry"

During the time of slavery and Jim Crow, nigger (pronounced nigga by many of the Afrikans, and bigoted southerners) was the acknowledged descriptive for Afrikan peoples. Afrikans internalized the pain of this word and eventually learned to identify with it as a self-referential term; which simultaneously planted the subliminal seeds of racial inferiority. Nigga (Nigger), each time it is encouraged as a self-referential term, it reinforces White supremacy; and Caucasian curses upon Afrikans become self-fulfilling prophesiers.

Freedom Is Highly Contagious and Very Infectious

Freedom is in all probability one of the most infectious psychological and physiological contagions ever to be experienced by humankind. No matter the situation or the circumstance, the enslaved and oppressed will always contract this contagion of freedom and aspire to be as free as, or freer than their captors. Men and women which come into contact with this contagion will unquestionably be affected, by this infections' contagious consequence; by exhibiting symptoms of rebellious thoughts, rebellious speech and rebellious actions. Freedom infects and inspires all who come into contact with it; demanding they aspire to be free.

As Afrikan people began to understand the fact that, the names of all other races associated those people with historical references and historical land masses, which in turn revealed to them their historical origins and provided them with a sense of identity; they began to comprehend the consequences of not taking on cultural and historical identities. When you don't know your history, or where you come from; best believe that someone will invent a history which includes you; create a culture for you, and concoct *your* genesis.

Now understanding that racial identities mattered, Afrikan people began to search out their true racial and cultural identities. Regrettably, Afrikan' endeavors to discover and acquire their true identities are always fraught with opposition from both outside and within the race; due to the agenda of the racists and due to the involuntary conditioning of their Afrikan slaves. Consequently, Afrikans cultural and identity evolution encompasses Afrikans devolving into slaves, niggers, coons, spooks, spades, coloreds, Negroes, Blacks and Afrikan-Americans. Now with the advent of nigga, Afrikans are poised to de-evolve back into niggers.

Black became the acceptable and selected terminology for the racial and cultural designation, for people of Afrikan ancestry in the late 1960s and early 1970s. In the mid 1970s, the term Afro-American came to be the standard term to be utilized in the description of Afrikan peoples, and now at this moment, African-American appears to be the description of choice. The idiom African-American (as a racial designation), subliminally suggests that, Afrikan people in America had no noteworthy histories, prior to their arrival in America.

As *Afro-Americans,* Black peoples' racial identities equated their origins to a contemporary hair style. The Afro! The short lived *Afro-American,* as a racial designation, was subsequently progressively replaced by the more politically accurate term *African-American,* in the early 1990s. Conversely, the racial descriptive *Black* presently (disappointingly) continues to be the most widespread, and most commonly utilized racial designation for people of Afrikan ancestry.

The Art Of Uncle Tomming; For Fear of Massa's Wrath

Afrikan slaves often surrendered to racist assumptions about niggers by using the term to their advantage utilizing the self-deprecatory deception of Tomming. Implicit in so doing, was the unspoken reminder that a presumed inherently morally, or intellectually inferior person, or "subhuman in essence," a nigger could not reasonably be held responsible for work performed incorrectly, an *accidental* fire in the kitchen, or any other similar offenses. It was a means of deflecting responsibility in the hope of escaping the wrath of an overseer or master. Its use as a self-referential term was also a way to avoid suspicion and put Whites at ease. A slave who referred to himself or another Black as a *nigga* presumably accepted the subordinate role that was his unfortunate lot and, therefore, posed no threat to white authority.

"S. L. A. V. E."

*(***S***tolen,* **L***ost,* **A***nd,* **V***iciously,* **E***duKKKated)*

The stolen children of conquered peoples,
Stolen, **L**ost, **A**nd, **V**iciously, **E**duKKKated,
MiseduKKKated, segregated, isolated and re-created!

A new creation,
A re-creation for their recreation,
For the destruction of an African Nation!

Re-created in a foreign land,
Re-created by the White Man,
Re-created to be his right hand,
Yes, Niggers are the White Man's right hand,
Used, abused and kept confused!

Trained like beasts,
And kept on a leash,
To protect his (stolen) land,
To protect his (sickly) health,
To protect his (stolen) wealth,
To protect his (abused) Wife,
To protect his (immoral) life!

MiseduKKKated with a shrewd intelligence,
Kept submerged in a blissful ignorance,
To function *normally* in total subservience!

No longer shackled in chains of old,
Now symbolically shackled in chains of gold,
You've sold your self; you've sold your soul,
You kill your own, to get their (stolen) gold,

Remember.......

"All that glitters isn't gold!"
Is their (stolen) gold worth your soul?

MiseduKKKation, segregation and isolation,
This is their formula for your re-creation,
This is their formula for your incarceration in a racist nation,
This is their formula that made you a "SLAVE" fearing emancipation!

Nigger, haven't you figured,
That, that which made you a **S.L.A.V.E.**
Makes you a Nigger?
Can it be that hard to figure?
That a SLAVE is a nigger, nigga?

Stolen, **L**ost, **A**nd, **V**iciously, **E**duKKKated!

"Mustafa Rasul Al-Amin"
(121694)

Ending All Confusion

The words nigger and nigga are the same and share the same unchanged historical definitions. Southern and Afrikan-American dialects in this country have traditionally changed the, *err* sound with the, *uh* sound.

Originally, the word nigger, as it pertains to people of Afrikan ancestry, was created by bigoted racists, to be a debilitating, dehumanizing, xenophobic descriptive, for all people of Afrikan ancestry. By design, the word nigger was fashioned to be a debilitating and humiliating adjective, manufactured with the intentions of robbing Afrikan peoples completely, of their dignity, their humanity, their personalities and their Afrikan souls! The word nigger was fashioned with the intention of transforming and re-creating Afrikan peoples.

Along the way, as an additional bonus, something very predictable and very interesting transpired. This despicable descriptive, this abominable adjective took on an entirely new function, and its true intentions were made manifest. The word usurped the life out of Afrikans and the power out of Afrika, assuming a powerful and transformative, life of its own. Niggers became living breathing re-creations of the racists.

The word metamorphosed its victims' mentalities, into newly developed fabrications and new versions of human-beings, and mentally and physically changed them into illogical, backwards thinking niggers. The word nigger evolved into an actual being, or should I say that, some Black people seem to be, beginning to evolve mentally and physically, into new and more abominable versions of this contemptible adjective. Consequently, new niggers are being born everyday, attempting to hide behind the façade of new niggas.

Unforeseen to many of the word's sufferers, the word's intention was not to, merely redefine the Afrikans, but to completely and thoroughly reconstruct the Afrikans mentally, physically, and spiritually, into one of the most vile abominations, that the world has yet to witness. Niggers were created and utilized with the conscious and premeditated intentions, of transforming and re-creating Afrikan peoples as justification for Afrikan incarceration, and for the benefit of Caucasians; whilst being a detriment to their Afrikan selves.

When you commence to truly comprehend the evolutionary process, you begin to understand the fact that environmental stresses, both external and internal, do in fact contribute significantly as factors in the roles of all humans' evolutionary development. What we eat and drink, how we function, our environments and even how we think are all contributory to the evolutionary developmental processes of all peoples.

So as you should now see, it is very much possible to re-create a people by manipulating environments to affect evolutionary development. Human engineering is not just some whimsical science fiction, fairy tale watched on television. Human engineering are very real experiments, and ***"projects"*** (hint, wink, wink,). Do you get it my niggers? Contemporary niggers and niggas are the results of evolutionary engineering.

To end the confusion, we must recognize, acknowledge and comprehend the truth as it becomes relevant to the existence of niggers. We must attain the ability to honestly and unashamedly realize the fact based realities of the existence of niggers. Once we acquire these capabilities we subsequently concentrate our strengths, our energies and all our collective geniuses, into the direction of eradicating niggers and niggas from our psyches and our existences; thus taking the nigger and nigga problems out of our communities.

Yes, niggas do exist. Niggas are real. Niggas are very much tangible. Niggas in truth do physically exist and every people on this Earth, too include Afrikans, associate the words nigga and nigger by definition to Afrikan people. Whenever and wherever nigga is spoken, written or sang; all know that it is referencing people of Afrikan ancestry. There is no such thing as Chinese niggers, Indian niggers, Mexican niggers, or Caucasian or White niggers (White nigger is an oxymoron).

Niggas are the iniquitous creations of wicked White men's imaginations. Accordingly, niggas are wicked by their fundamental natures, as they are spawned from the deepest, darkest, vile recesses of iniquitous imaginations. Niggers were conceived through depraved, sadistic acts of violence, rape, incest, slavery, oppression and murder. Niggas are both the victims and the wicked result of centuries of psychological abuses and physical abuses, which by design, deliberately created a self destructively suicidal creature.

"Niggers Do Exist"
(Yes Niggas Do Exist)

Niggers do exist!

As Afrikan People we can no longer deny the reality that real live niggers do exist,
Because when you show a nigger that, "niggers are a myth and really don't truly exist!"
Niggers will insist, "Nigga we do exist!" Get pissed, resist, and might strike you with their fist!

Tell a nigger and show a nigger that a nigger is a racist's creation of detriment!
Teach a nigger and preach to a nigger that niggers are a psychotic contaminant!
Take a nigger, talk to a nigger and prove that niggers are a product of confinement!
And a nigger will attack your argument telling you that niggas are a term of endearment!

I'm truly astounded and dumbfounded to learn that niggers do truly exist,
And I'm even more amazed and astonished to learn that niggers proudly exist,
As Afrikan People we can no longer deny the reality that real live niggers do exist,
Because when you show a nigger that, "niggers are a myth and really don't truly exist!"
Niggers will insist, "Nigga we do exist!" Get pissed, resist, and might strike you with their fist!

Niggers were born in a racist, slave owning, White Man's imagination,
This means that niggers are a racist creation and a Caucasian creation,
The frightened, weak and ignorant Brothers and Sisters on Massas' plantations,
Who submitted to Massa and passed their cowardice on down; to future generations!

Niggers are psychology programmed to be self hating and self exacerbating,
And niggers lust for, and love their enemies, who they're constantly imitating,
Pathological niggers suppose that everything Caucasian is worth celebrating,
And niggers suffer from a psycho-pathology; that is detrimentally devastating!

Originally "named" nigger by racist White Men to make the Afrikan be inhuman,
Niggers were legally classified "beasts of burden" made to be three fifths a man,
Niggers would routinely and insanely accept being niggers, and less than human,
Insane, inhumane niggers are now viewed by the world as bestial burdens of man!

Niggers are unconcerned with humanity and are all consumed with vanity!
Niggers are unconcerned with God and spirituality being all consumed monetarily!
Niggers are unconcerned with truth and reality choosing instead to exist in White mythology!
Niggers stripped of their personalities and humanity function dysfunctional in orchestrated insanity!

Tell a nigger and show a nigger that a nigger is a racist's creation of detriment!
Teach a nigger and preach to a nigger that niggers are a psychotic contaminant!
Take a nigger, talk to a nigger and prove that niggers are a product of confinement!
And a nigger will attack your argument telling you that niggas are a term of endearment!

So you see my niggas.......
Niggers do exist!

As Afrikan People we can no longer deny the reality that real live niggers do exist,
Because when you show a nigger that, "niggers are a myth and really don't truly exist!"
Niggers will insist, "Nigga we do exist!" Get pissed, resist, and might strike you with their fist!

Yes my niggers; you niggas do exist.

"Mustafa Rasul Al-Amin"
(082401)

Nigger Bits and Media Bytes

While nigga raises comparatively few objections when utilized by Black rappers, it is generally considered to be off-limits to non-Black performers, with increasingly rare exceptions:

The Beastie Boys, an all-white hip-hop group, were forced off-stage subsequent to utilizing the word in a non-hostile context to refer to their audience.

In 2001, Latino performer Jennifer Lopez provoked the rage of the Afrikan-American community when she used the word in a song written by two Black songwriters on the TODAY Show.

Black comedian Chris Rock's 1996 television broadcast, "Bring The Pain" and 1997 album "Roll With The New," included a segment known as "Niggas vs. Black People," which humorously describes the behavior of a number of Blacks that adhere to the nigger stereotype. Rock describes "niggas" as "low-expectation-having'" individuals -- proud to be ignorant, violent, and on welfare- the equivalent of "White trash." The controversy of this too exasperated many because they felt it surrendered to anti-Black racism, and it led Rock's decision to quit performing that particular skit.

On the other hand, a portion of the repertoire of Caucasian-American comedian George Carlin is his routine concerning sensitive words - which words by themselves are never good or bad and it is the user's intention that counts. "We don't mind when Richard Pryor or Eddie Murphy uses it," he quips. "Why? Because we know they're not racists. They're Niggers!"

Since the coining of the phrase "the N-word," some television broadcasters have added the word nigger retroactively, to their lists of taboo words, thereby censoring many movies and television programs from the past in which the word is used, no matter what context, or the consequence on the program. For example:

The television broadcasts of the motion picture "Die Hare With A Vengeance" which originally featured a White character being placed in jeopardy when he is forced to carry a sign saying, "I hate niggers" around Harlem; are altered so that the sign now says "I hate everybody," which is not offensive and, critics argue, renders the scene far less effective.

Mel Brook's anti-racism comedy "Blazing Saddles" is rarely shown on American commercial television anymore due to the pervasive use of the word.

African-American comedian Dave Chapelle has frequently utilized the word in satire. In the first season of "The Chapelle Show," a blind White supremacist, unaware of the fact that he was Black, utilizes the word repeatedly in remarks disparaging Black people, and then, at the end of the sketch comments that he left his wife because she is a "nigger-lover". In the second season of the show, Dave Chapelle exploited this word even more with the sketch, "The Niggar Family," which a portrayed a 1950s White family with a last name resembling the infamous word. The comedy pivots upon the interaction among other members of the community and results in an uncensored and buffoonish outcome.

The controversial animated series The Boondocks (television series which airs on The Cartoon Network) frequently uses the word "Nigga" by the main characters and sometimes others. The term can be used to shock the other characters, or for satirical purposes, as when Granddad tells Huey not to use the word in his house, Huey reminds him that he himself used the word 46 times the day before. Granddad's reply is "Nigga hush!" The show also makes note of "Nigga Moments", where an otherwise well-adjusted Black man or woman acts in an ignorant or self-destructive way out of anger; on the Cartoon Channel.

Nigger In The Window: A book written by a young black girl describing the world from her window.

To sell a book comedian and activist Dick Gregory titled it: NIGGER

Never Ignorant Getting Goals Accomplished

(Tupac Shakur's Acronym for Nigga)

Niggas are people of Afrikan ancestry who have been re-created to be ignorant as it pertains to who they are, and from whence they came. Niggers are apathetically and impudently uninformed of their histories, condescendingly apathetic to contemporary concerns, and shamelessly unconcerned about their futures. Fundamentally; niggers are prime examples of suicidal manifestations. Niggas are perfidious, disruptive and antagonistically detrimental towards their own people and causes. A nigga (nigger) is a S.L.A.V.E.

"The Nigga Incantation"

And, they chant, "Nigga, Nigga, Nigga" as they ignorantly internalize negativity,
Ignorantly believing that, internalized negativities will increase Black popularity,
Renamed nigga, and recreated nigga, by enemies which keep them in captivity,
Niggas now believe, that internalized negativity will increase Black productivity,
As the descendants of Slaves ignorantly celebrate the curse of Afrikan slavery!

"Mustafa Rasul Al-Amin"
(Sunday May 28, 2006)

As they embrace the commercialization of niggas, "Remember how they used to commercialize niggers?" Histories unlearned are histories repeated.

The N-Word

A euphemism is a word or phrase utilized in place of a term or word, which might be considered to direct, harsh, unpleasant or offensive. *The N-Word* is the euphemism for the words nigger or nigga.

This euphemism became a part of the American lexicon, during the racially divisive trial of retired football player O.J. Simpson, who was prosecuted with, and subsequently acquitted of the much criticized, widely televised, and highly publicized double homicide of two Caucasians. This case would be overwhelmingly affected by the Caucasian utilization of the word nigger.

The prosecution's key witness was Los Angles police detective Mark Fuhrman, who at the outset denied ever using the racial slur. But, the discovery of tape recordings with Detective Fuhrman vigorously using the racial slur brought his credibility into question. An aspiring screenwriter named Laura McKinney made the recordings. In 1985 she was working on a screenplay with regard to women in the police department, and according to Mark Fuhrman, he was using the word as part of his "bad-cop" persona.

Members of the media reporting on and discussing Fuhrman's testimony began utilizing the euphemism, "the N-word" instead of repeating the actual profanity, presumably as a way to avoid offending both their audiences and advertisers. The euphemism was adopted quickly by American society as a way to avoid uttering one of the most generally offensive words in the English language.

Wiggers Whiggers Or Wiggas

The term wigger/whigger refers to White mimickers of certain nigger behaviors and affectations of hip-hop and thug cultures. It is a "portmanteau word (look it up)" of white and nigger. Logically the word should to be considered offensive to Afrikans on account of its connection to the word nigger and because the word is reflective of stereotypical notions about Black people. However, some people have now embraced the utilization of the word and have found the word to be entertaining by nature. Similarly, other portmanteau words were formed from nigger, and should as well be considered offensive in nature, even when used to describe the intra-groups of others (i.e. Chinese niggers; chiggers or chiggas).

History has continuously invalidated the illogical notions that, persistently utilizing this word will eventually rob it of its destructive power. Like of so many of the other iniquitous words in the language, though used regularly, they remain offensive in most contexts, and the word nigga is no exception. It also retains its all too sinister meanings. Nigger is a word that needs to be placed in a category with the worst words, in the history of the world's language. No matter how much the word nigger is utilized it is still just as hurtful.

Simply because people become desensitized to the word, this does not mean that it loses its power, or its meaning. We exist in cultures which are inundated in violence. Violence is in our neighborhoods, in our newspapers, in our schools, on television, in our music, and in the video games. Oftentimes, many of us see so much violence that they become desensitized to it, and see nothing wrong with the inhumanity of violence being perpetrated against another; as they subliminally eternalize and act out violent behaviors.

Similarly, the repetitive usages of the word nigger may make its use more common but, devastating none the less. Repetitive usages of the word only serve to make the word more camouflaged; as the carnages caused by the word increases tenfold. Repetitive usage not only desensitizes but also dehumanizes us.

A nigger is a nigga is a nigger

Recently, a high school English teacher called one of his Afrikan-American students', nigga. The teacher maintained that it was not a racial slur, because of his enunciation and his pronunciation of the word. The teacher asserted that, because he said, "nigga" and not "nigger," that makes the word not be any sort of racial slur. The teacher went on to justify his use of the word saying, *"They always use this word among themselves."*

The truth of this matter is; as a high school English teacher, this teacher was conscious in his knowledge that phonetically speaking, many Afrikan-Americans, because of their cultural and intellectual upbringings and our inherent African dialects, we regularly enunciate particular words differently than our Caucasian-American counterparts. Frequently we replace the "er" sounds with the "uh" sounds (i.e. stopper, stoppa, Hilfiger, Hilfiga or Hilfinga, proper, propa, singer, sanga, sister, sista, brother, brotha, nigger, nigga). Do pronunciations and enunciations change definitions? "As little Riley of The Boondocks puts it, *"White people - say - thee - whole-la - word-da."*

"Volunteer Slaves"

Too many Brothers and Sisters are ignorantly caught up in the prison industry,
Not realizing that this industry is nothing more than another name for slavery,
Not realizing that this industry is nothing more than another game of slavery,
They foolishly and ignorantly deem it a rite of passage as an act of bravery!

To surrender;
Is to volunteer for slavery,
And this is not an act of bravery!

"Mustafa Rasul Al-Amin"
(032201)

(CHAPTER Five)

"RACISM"

Racism:

1) A belief in the superiority of a particular race, because of race.

2) The theory and belief that human abilities, behaviors, capabilities, etc, are determined by race.

Since the words racism and racist are so regularly and frivolously bandied about in our daily discussions, I feel that it is long past time we plainly discussed, and defined these words, to end our confusions about these words, whilst examining the true affects of these words, and what effect they have upon us.

Simply put, racism is nothing more than the belief, that race is the causation for human behavior. In other words, racism is the belief that skin color (or race) makes people act a certain way, perform a certain way, think in certain ways, and speak in a certain way. Understanding these definitions of racism, anyone who subscribes to these beliefs must be viewed as a racist. Furthermore, subsequent to a thoroughly truthful investigation (much to Blacks' chagrin), we discover that people of Afrikan descent have become and are beginning to be, even more racist than their Caucasian counterparts. We must constantly remember that racism is a concocted belief invented in the iniquitous minds of wicked men, and is being presently being used to reinforce and strengthen White supremacy. Racism is nothing more than a wicked untrue belief.

Racism is the psychological mechanism which exalts one particular race of people to believe that they are greater than all other races of people. Racism at its outset is a side-effect of peoples' racial insecurities, which to a certain extent; most likely find its genesis in the evolutionary migration of Afrikans out of Afrika and into Europe, and in the evolutionary process, which ultimately transformed the migrating Afrikans into the European Caucasians. The following is an excerpt written by the late great Dr. John Henrik Clarke;

Now with the coming of the European to power in the world, because of his sickness and insecurity, not only Africa ran into trouble, but the world found itself in trouble to the extent that we left the cultural base of our creation and became an imitator of someone else's concept of culture.

Now, let's tell about how the Africans, the Asians and the people of warmer climates celebrated the force of nature and how the Europeans tried to fight the force of nature. In Europe, nature was unkind. There was all that snow for three or four months which did not allow enough time to plant, to harvest and to store.

And so, the European was angry with nature for not giving him enough time to survive. But, in Africa, nature was kind and sends fruits and vegetables every season. In Africa, nature also sends fish all year round; while in Europe, the ponds are frozen and there is a limited time when you can fish or store.

So the Europeans developed an attitude toward nature that is defiant, while the Africans and other people in warmer climates developed an attitude toward nature that made them celebrate the bountifulness of nature. The African would celebrate the harvest all year round. He would celebrate birth, and he would celebrate death as a continuation of life.

"Dr. John Henrik Clarke"
(Ceremony And Celebration In African Society)

Racism Is a Side-Effect of Evolutionary Insecurity

When a people's origins are of hostile environments, more than likely, those people will be hostile people. When a people's origins are of environments that are conducive to aggressive, dominator type behaviors; aggressive mentalities become a side-effect of their evolutionary development and those people will more than likely to develop into aggressive, hostile, and dominating people. Aggressive, dominating people are not a sharing people. They subscribe to the tenets of, "Only the strong shall survive," and, "It's a dog eat dog world." The insecurities developed in their minds will manifest; and ascribe to the tenants of racism.

Understanding the psychological temperaments of Caucasians is crucial, and very necessary for our own liberation and advancement. Understanding that Caucasians have conquered the world is a fundamental and crucial point which must be completely understood before we can really be liberated. Understanding the Caucasians' insecurities and the causations for those insecurities cannot be ignored and must fully be explored and absolutely understood so, we can know exactly who and what Afrikans are dealing with.

And to conclude, Afrikans must absolutely understand and acknowledge our own psychological limitations and inadequacies in efforts to counteract any countermeasures which will be put into action, against us in our pursuit of liberation. We must first recognize that we are damaged, understand how we are damaged and honestly acknowledge the extent of the damage, before we can fix the damage. Everywhere you find ideologies of racial disparity and racial supremacy; xenophobic Caucasians vigilantly sustain a presence.

Subsequent to completion of our investigation, we discover that the entire world has been touched by and affected by Caucasian domination. In every culture that Caucasians have touched, a wake of racism that promotes and strengthens White supremacy will always be evidenced; as their theories of racism abound.

Racism As It Pertains To Afrikan People

One of the first questions asked by the majority of people is, "Why does racism so overwhelmingly appear to affect people of Afrikan ancestry more than any other people?" The simple answer; xenophobic people fear genetic domination. The xenophobes view Afrikans as a genetic threat, which possess the capability to breed them into extinction. This is the reason so many Black men were castrated during their lynching when lynching was AmeriKKKa's favorite pastime. To this day Afrikan genetics is the principal fear of the racists. Caucasians' fear of Afrikan genetics so great that, they even passed legislation which determined the amount of Afrikan blood it took to classify one to be Negroid (nigger); in efforts to keep their race pure.

In actuality many other races of people darker than the racists, have as well, been crushingly affected by the racial insecurities of Caucasians. For example, groups like the Native Americans, and the Indians of India were completely conquered and subjugated, by the malevolent bigoted activities of their Caucasian conquerors. Racism and racial manipulations have thoroughly confused the South American inhabitants of that continent, and made extinct the original inhabitants of the North American continent.

Racism is a psychological phenomenon based upon theoretic conjecture, meaning racism is an emotional element which is a result of a suspicious people's inherent insecurities, brought about by their xenophobic paranoia. Caucasians have harnessed the power of their psychological dysfunctions and now utilize it for purposes of maintaining complete supremacy, over all other races. Caucasians then and now use racism to make Afrikans appear less than human and to keep them in the roles of secondary citizens, demanding that, the world view Afrikans as divinely cursed, ethnic abnormalities. Christian religions and manipulated biblical scripture only serve to reinforce and strengthen their counterfeited, divine justifications for racism.

Caucasians arrived on the continent of Afrika and used racial misinformation (racism) to reclassify and to dehumanize Afrikan peoples by means of camouflaged, premeditative intentions of conquering them and enslaving them. When Caucasians entered into Afrika, Afrikans were wholeheartedly, ready to share the wealth but, as stated previously in this writing, "Aggressive, dominating people are not a sharing people." It has constantly been proven time and time again that, Caucasians take whatever it is that they lust for, too include the lives and souls of human beings. White supremacy bases its foundation upon domination.

People also ask, "Why do Black people continuously complain about racism; claiming to be the victims of racism?" Because racism does exist, and is relentlessly being carried out primarily against Black people. Logically, those whom racism affects the greatest, will complain the most, and be most boisterous. It is a matter of simple logic.

Many will state that, life has tremendously improved for Afrikan-Americans. While this may be correct, the reality of this situation is that, life has tremendously improved for everyone due to technological advances but; by the same indication those same people will admit that racism does still exist and for Afrikan people racism does still remain a significant problem. Racism today is more deceitfully sophisticated and put into practice with more surreptitious approaches. Today's trickery is to implement racialist tactics in a manner in which it makes the victims look as if they are victimizing themselves.

Blame The Victim Tactics

For the most part, Afrikans in America have no control over the media. As a consequence, Afrikans have no control over the images that the racists portray to the world. They create dysfunctional and fabricated images which glorify dysfunction, drugs and violence, constantly replaying these images until all who view them, believes them to be truth. Their continuous glorification of these images makes the victims of these images appear to perceive them as admirable and advantageous, while other people distinguish them as disadvantageous, sickening and reprehensible. The new plan of the racists is to exterminate our children before they even had a chance to grow. Train them up to be self-destructive and they will be destructive.

Similar to a loaded gun, those racists in control aim dysfunctional images towards the hearts and minds of the young and immature people, of the victimized race, in glorified manners. The racists teach the young that these dysfunctional behaviors are virtuous normalcies, amongst Afrikan people. Daily bombarded by media print, movies, music, video games, and a multitude of other reinforcing edifying apparatuses, which by design encourage our youth surrender to these dysfunctional notions; as intended, many do surrender to these pseudo-subliminal messages, and grow into the dysfunctional adults, that they were meant to be. And then by design, the victimized are blamed for own their victimization, dysfunctional socialization, and detrimental behaviors. Premeditated dysfunctional socialization often disguised as cultural identifications.

Why Are Afrikans The Primary Victims Of Racism?

When discussing racism, we must always remember that racism emanates from the mindset of insecurity. Insecurity is a form of fear, and Caucasians harbor numerous fears when it pertains to people of Afrikan ancestry. When it comes to the Caucasians' concerns, about people of Afrikan ancestry, there are three fundamental fears that actually worry racist Caucasians. Their biggest fear is the fear of being bred into non-existence. Then there is their fear of becoming a minority within the country. And last but not least, Caucasians fear losing control and domination over the world and those people existing within the world. Consequently, to maintain control they keep Afrikans confused, divided and alienated from the world and each other. The divide and conquer thing seems to always work.

(Xenophobia – fear of strangers)

When things go wrong in a society, the people at the bottom are held responsible for all the wrongs of the society. Afrikans' skin color makes people of Afrikan ancestry the obvious targets of people in Caucasian dominated societal structures. Subsequent to the completion of any truthful investigation we will find that, darker skin people are ceaselessly fending off racial attacks from the rest of the world. Racial paradigms are designed to be orchestrated from the top of society, executed by the middle of society, and devastate the bottom of the society. Racism dictates; Black skin shall forever be on the bottom wrung of society.

Like the men of each race of people, Afrikan men as a rule, are generally considered to be representative of the strengths of their people. Caucasians' racially offensive attacks are logically aimed at, and focused on, Afrikan men. This is why every facet of Caucasian controlled mediums is concerned with, the cultural investigation, and character assassination of Black males. As an example, Germany victimized its Jewish people first targeting males; and America has for centuries victimized and vilified Afrikan-American males.

Afrikans' vilification becomes their racial justifications for our incarceration and our assassinations, in their ethnically slanted and prejudiced nations. Nevertheless, racism could not have become as fundamentally powerful as it has without the supportive and cooperative thoughts in the fundamental tenets of racism; by both the oppressors and the oppressed.

Who Are The Racists Supportive And Cooperative Of The Fundamental Tenets Of Racism?

When the concern is racism, everybody vehemently and innocently claims not to be racist but, their words and actions prove different. Undeniably, the majority of Caucasians are indeed racists, who daily practice racism. As stated, racial paradigms are orchestrated from the top of a society, executed by the middle of the society, with the intention of destroying the bottom of the society. Racial plans and programs, are put into place by those legislators and leaders at the upper echelon of every society, and are implemented by those who exist in the lower echelons of those societies, to control those at the bottom of those societies.

However (and most unfortunate), Black people are some of the most pathetic racists in existence. Black people are perhaps (ignorantly) the most egregious racists on this planet. Yes, you read this right! Black people, people of Afrikan ancestry, are ignorantly, the most egregious racists in the history of this planet!

Whenever I tell this truth, inevitably someone will ask, "How can Black people be racists?" I've even read somewhere, were some of our scholarly types wrote that, "Black people can't be racists, because they do not have enough power to be racists." In their *unscientific* manner of thinking, only those people in power and in control of the society can be racists or put into practice, the tenets of racism. However, once again I remind you of the true definition of racism. Simply put, racism is nothing more than the belief, that race is the causation for human behavior, and anyone who surrenders to this belief and its tenets is a racist.

Whenever we engage into conversations with the majority Black of people, regrettably their conversations will eventually replicate learned, stereotypical beliefs in which they have been taught, and assimilated into concocted Black cultures. Black people tend to continually speak the words and phrases, which correlate dysfunctional behaviors as cultural Black normalities; surrendering to the conquering tenets of racism.

When White people are called Wiggers, this is an inexcusable, transparent act of racism. The implication is that Whites are imitating niggers. When people presume that all Black people excel at sports, sing and dance, rap, are sexually promiscuous, abandon their children or submit to any type of stereotype because of race, then they are racists. Unfortunately, far too many Black people see, hear, acknowledge and daily surrender to and accept these detrimental and dangerous racial stereotypes as cultural normalities.

Time and again, I hear Black people saying things like, "He doesn't act Black, or she doesn't act Black, or those White people act so Black." Just what is acting Black? Acting Black is simply defined as submitting to dysfunctional, stereotypical behaviors of buffoonery, created by the racists with the intention to demean and lessen the humanness' of Afrikan peoples. When Black people start to eternalize these bogus beliefs as their realities, and began to espouse these counterfeit cultural convictions; they become conspiratorial, and complicit in the crime being perpetrated against Afrikan people, which makes them racists.

Black conversations which equate Black dysfunction to Black normalcy are conversations, which illustrate Black people's level of racism. When Afrikan people reiterate racially concocted phrases, they perpetuate stereotypical mythologies and promote stereotypical behaviors. When people start to promote mythology and perpetuate dysfunction, their children soon begin to think that art is imitating life, when in actuality life is imitating the racists' very real ability to manipulate people to be negative, and function dysfunctional.

How many times have we heard Black people saying things like, "You know that chicken ain't safe around Black people?" How often do we hear Back people bragging about the ostensibly natural athleticism, and sexual prowess of Black people? How often do we hear them faultily claim stereotypical, or dysfunctional criminal acts (packaged as street knowledge), the silly idea of incarceration as a rite of passage for Black men, or idiotically ridicule our natural appearances (Afrikan peoples' hair, lips and noses)? These actions are undeniable demonstrative signs of racism; and we become racists when we surrender to this thinking.

Racism is embracing racially dysfunctional stereotypes about Black people, which have been invented by White people, in which Black people have thoughtlessly, unknowingly and unintentionally surrendered to.

Racism is merely a belief that race is a causation for human behavior. Racism is a belief that race makes people act a certain way, perform a certain way and think in certain ways. Conscious knowledge of these definitions of racism demand subscribers of and surrenders to these beliefs; must be viewed as a racists.

Stockholm's Syndrome is the condition experienced by some people who have been held as hostages for extensive periods of time, in which they begin to identify with, and feel sympathetic towards their captors. Afrikans in America have taken Stockholm's Syndrome to a whole, another level. After over 400 years of Caucasian captivity; when one is cognizant of this psychological phenomenon, none should be surprised at the fact that traumatized Afrikans suffer immensely from this condition. Because of the consequences of Stockholm's Syndrome Black racism persuades the majority of Black people to completely identify with their Caucasian captors and oppressors. It has often been said, "If you lie down with dogs you will get up with fleas." We have most definitely lain down with the dogs and rose up with a serious gaggle of fleas.

Black racism influences Black people to assimilate Caucasian traditions and aspire to Caucasian realities. Afrikans' assimilation of Caucasian customs, traditions, and mannerisms is so extreme; that many Blacks now despise any Afrikan references, which may conjure up Afrikan images of God, and loathe the Afrikan standard of beauty bestowed upon them by God almighty. Many instead desire to resemble their captors, enslavers and oppressors. Limp straight hair, multicolored eyes, and willowy facial features have become lustful, desirous preferences, and their new standard of beauty, for Black people of Afrikan ancestry.

Afrikans' racist beliefs have transformed Afrikans into honorary Caucasians. Physically, they are Afrikans however; psychologically they are the embodiment of Caucasians. Yet, when people bring forth the issue of self-hatred, not understanding that they are Afrikan, many promptly let everybody know that they do not hate themselves, and that they in fact love themselves. This is the dilemma; many of us face when we try to address the issue of self-hatred; when many don't truly understand. We must begin to understand that, in these Black people's minds they are mutations and not Afrikans. Physically they are Black, but in their minds, psychologically they are Caucasian in thought. Those Black people accused of self-hatred must somehow, begin to understand the errors in their thinking. *You don't see colors?* The racists do! Liars!

Those Afrikans, who dare place the charge of racism, must begin to understand the true implication of the word racism; understanding that subscribers and surrenders to these beliefs; must be viewed as a racists. Those Blacks who stand accused of self-hatred must be made to understand that their racial designations are indeed Afrikan, and their loathing of Afrikans is nothing short of self-hatred and racism turned inward.

"Mustafa Rasul Al-Amin"
(Thursday July 24, 2008)

"I think an overwhelming portion of the intensely demonstrated animosity toward President Barack Obama is based on the fact that he is a Black man, that he's African-American. I live in the South, and I've seen the South come a long way, and I've seen the rest of the country that shared the South's attitude toward minority groups, particularly African-Americans."

"That racism inclination still exists, and I think it's bubbled up to the surface because of a belief among many White people, not just in the South but around the country, that African-Americans are not qualified to lead this great country. It is an abominable circumstance, and it grieves me and concerns me very deeply."

"Former President Jimmy Carter"
(September 16, 2009)

Chapter Six

"Eugenics"
(Building Bigger Better Benign Niggers)

Eugenics:

Selective breeding as proposed human improvement: the proposed improvement of the human species by encouraging or permitting reproduction of only those people with genetic characteristics judged desirable. Eugenics has been regarded with disfavor since the Nazi period.

Encarta Dictionary

The purpose of this essay is to demonstrate to Afrikan people how Caucasian people calculatingly set out to rob Afrikan people of their humanity; transforming them from humans into things; creating a sub-human that they would name, and issue the phony scientific descriptive of nigger. Out of ignorance, far too many are now accepting the moniker, and being daily duped into accepting faux cultural roles which reflect both buffoonery and dysfunction. People must begin to understand the fundamental and intricate mechanisms involved in the process of dehumanization. They must begin to recognize that it is a process which seeks out justifications to strip them of their humanity and basic human rights, often through ersatz science, and bogus religions and religious beliefs; to justify incarceration, occupation, extermination, and annihilation.

It is working! Hundreds of years ago, a plan of dehumanization was established to change Afrikan people into beings, which are less than human, and these individuals would be recognized as niggers. Programs and plans which utilize the science of eugenics were implemented to completely change, restructure, and recreate Afrikan people mentally, physically and spiritually. The objective of the plan was to dehumanize, Afrikans and breed them as objects; making bigger, stronger and more obedient things (niggers) to serve as a servant-class of animalistic beings, to work for, to strengthen, and to benefit of the dominant culture.

Eugenics is the applied science or socio-biological movement which promotes the use of practices aimed at changing the psychological, sociological, and genetic compositions of a population; usually referring to (perceived) inferior human populations. Eugenics was widely popular early in AmeriKKKa's racial history; becoming even more popular after the passage of the "Slave Trade Act" by the British Parliament in 1807. Eugenics came under public scrutiny only after Adolph Hitler and the Nazi Party applied these techniques to Caucasoid Peoples. Eugenics is often used with the farming techniques (science) of animal husbandry.

Ever since the post Nazi period, both the public and the scientific communities have zealously associated eugenics with the Nazi abuses; such as racial hygiene, human experimentation, and the extermination of undesired Caucasoid population groups. However, many still fail to even acknowledge AmeriKKKa's role for those same horrific abuses against Afrikan peoples. AmeriKKKa implemented government sponsored policies and programs to dehumanize, enslave and psychologically destroy all peoples of Afrikan ancestry, while justifying the enslavement of them by way of ersatz collectives of societal and religious justifications.

It has continuously been said that, "A history unlearned will oftentimes lead to a people being doomed to repeat their history." Regrettably, far too many Afrikan people choose to pay no attention to their history, and choose to outright reject their history; doomed to continuously repeat it! Since many Afrikans do not know their history or understand their history, many do not realize that they are daily reliving their history; caught up in devastating cycles of repetitiveness. Consequently, scores now recognize themselves to be niggers, and habitually gravitate towards disadvantageous behaviors and made-up cultures and customs which are both dysfunctional and detrimental to Afrikans as a people; moving them from people to things.

In The Beginning

The first indication of Afrikan slaves arriving in what is now presently acknowledged as The United States of America, was in 1526; over two centuries before the founding of The United States of America. These Afrikans were part of the San Miguel de Gualdape Colony, believed to be located in the Winyah Bay area of present day South Carolina; originated by the Spanish explorer Lucas Vásquez de Ayllón. The colony was almost straight away disbanded, after internal leadership struggles and slave revolts. Many of those slaves which escaped sought refuge amongst the local Native Americans. Lucas Vásquez de Ayllón and many of the colonists died of an epidemic, shortly after the founding of the colony in 1526, and the colony was abandoned leaving the escaped (Afrikans) slaves behind on the mysterious shores of North America.

The early 1600s was a time of war and empire-building in Southwest Africa. Portuguese traders under the rule of the king of Spain had established a colony, in Angola. The exporting of slaves to the Spanish New World had proved to be a profitable undertaking. So, the Portuguese waged war against the kingdoms of Ndongo and Kongo in the north, to capture and deport thousands of Afrikan men and women. The slaves (Afrikans) passed through a slave fortress at the port city of Luanda, which is still Angola's capital today.

From 1618 until 1620 the Portuguese fought the people of Ndongo in West Africa. Thousands of Afrikans were abducted and murdered by the Portuguese, African warlords, and numerous mercenaries employed by the Portuguese in Angola. Countless Afrikans were forcefully marched from their villages to the port of Luanda. Some escaped and many died. They were frequently kept in terrible conditions for months, until a predetermined quota of 350 to 400 could be captured, enslaved and crammed together on waiting ships to be transported on perilous voyages across the ocean to the mines of Mexico, and to the fields of Brazil.

The Portuguese had been in Angola for some time, building a large trade industry between Afrika, Europe and the New World. Portuguese law required all Afrikan slaves to be baptized and made *Christian* before being loaded onto ships. In 1619, slaves were loaded aboard the slave merchant ship *Sao Joao Bautista* and departed for Brazil and other harbors of the Spanish Indies when it encountered two pirate ships; *The White Lion* and *The Treasurer*, in the West Indies. During one of their pirating raids in the Caribbean, *The White Lion* and *The Treasurer* attacked *The Sao Joao Bautista* and seized portions of the cargo from *The Sao Joao Bautista*, which included many captured Angolan slaves. The captured Angolans were from the kingdoms of Ndongo and Kongo, and spoke the languages of the Bantu people of West Afrika.

Damaged from the battle and the more severely damaged in a immense storm; in August 1619 *The White Lion* landed just outside Jamestown, Virginia at *Point Comfort* (presently recognized as Fort Monroe) with a cargo of slightly more than 20 Afrikans; seeking provisions, and help from the people of Virginia. These 20 plus Afrikans were listed on the ship's manifest as, *"20 and odd Negroes."* The *"20 and Odd Negroes"* would be the first *"recorded"* transaction of Afrikan slave trading in British colonial America. In 1619, more than a century before the founding of the United States of America, *The Afrikan Slave Trade* had officially commenced in America. A short time subsequent to the appearance of *The White Lion* in Point Comfort, Virginia, *The Treasurer* arrived carrying even more Afrikan Slaves, to sell to the colonists.

When *tobacco* became the main source of income for the colonists, the economic success of the colonies became dependent on the amount of tobacco produced. The growing of tobacco required much land and a large stable workforce to be prosperous. The increased demand for a large workforce, coupled with the availability of Afrikan slaves were both major contributing factors for the Afrikan's enslavement in America.

Consciously understanding that Afrikans were people, a justification had to be manufactured to justify the enslavement of fellow human beings. A rationalization had to be created to validate the incarceration and the enslavement of millions of human beings for the purpose of attaining free labor and a validation had to be contrived to rationalize one human being, owning another human being, as chattel (personal property).

To accomplish their monstrously grotesque justifications and rationalizations; many of man's fundamental humanistic systems of social development have been corrupted for the purpose of dehumanizing Afrikans, and justifying the enslavement of Afrikan people, unto other peoples. Dehumanization is their justification.

Dehumanization of Afrikans

Dehumanization is a psychological process whereby members of the dominant, oppressive group asserts the "inferiority" of the weaker group through subtle or overt acts and statements, promoting them as being less than human; void of any humanity and thus, not deserving of any moral or humanistic considerations.

In the case of Afrikan peoples; deceptive religions and religious doctrines, ersatz science, propagandized societal and social programs (to include the exploitation of media outlets), and legislative processes have been utilized and exploited for the purposes of dehumanizing Afrikan peoples. History is full of examples; from the misinterpretations of Biblical passages to the actual enactment and implementation of American laws which were created to dehumanize; and make chattel and *second class humans* of Afrikan people.

Historically, nigger is the name most associated with the creation of this newly dehumanized creature and the invocation of this wretched word nigger, to this day; invokes both conscious and subconscious images of lesser, dysfunctional human beings which are less competent, diseased, unclean, criminally dangerous and worthy of incarceration. Unfortunately, for many people of Afrikan descent, both the word nigger and the dysfunctional character, which acts out nigger stereotypes, are now both acceptable, and appropriate.

Carter G. Woodson once remarked, *"When you control a man's thinking you don't have to worry about his actions. You don't have to tell him not to stand here or go yonder. He will find his "proper place" and will stay in it. You don't need to send him to the back door. He will go without being told. In fact, if there is no back door, he will cut one for his special benefit."*

Centuries ago, slave traders, slave breeders, and slave owners once calculatingly set out to dehumanize and enslave Afrikan people mentally, physically and spiritually; and they would name their new creatures' niggers. To successfully bring this calculated plan to fruition not only would they have to substantiate the enslaving of a people to the oppressors' but; to more effectively enslave a people what better way is there to enslave a people other than justifying the enslavement to the enslaved? To accomplish this, one must control the thinking of the enslaved. When one control a person's thinking, they don't have to worry about their actions. One only has to reinterpret their characteristics, and their actions will become predictable.

Centuries ago, slave traders, slave breeders, and slave owners set out to produce a bigger, stronger, and more benign nigger. They wanted niggers that would be more physically adept and more psychologically and spiritually inept. Controlling the thinking of niggers is critical to accomplishing this feat, and becomes a perpetually self prophesizing process, which not only controls contemporary thinking, but future thinking and imagery, which contributes to the success of the dominant society, and the continuous subjugation of the enslaved (oppressed and suppressed) people. Niggers now go to the backdoor without being told to.

Currently, I watch African people (niggers) fulfilling the wishes of those racists of centuries ago; arrogantly accepting the moniker of nigger, lifting weights and building bigger, stronger bodies, whilst simultaneously ignoring, neglecting, and even assaulting their emotional, psychological and spiritual psyches; continually accepting propagandized, dysfunctional imagery, and counterfeit cultures, religions, science and histories as gospel, while chemically killing their minds and bodies, with foods and drugs, premeditatedly designed particularly for them. Soul food (pork based foods) premium whiskies and malt liquors are killing niggers!

When incarcerations becomes rites of passage, and nigger becomes a fraternal bond instead of the curse that it should naturally be; then it is absolute proof that the plans of the slave traders, slave breeders, and slave owners from centuries ago have come to fruition. When subjugated peoples manufacture nationally televised debates over the appropriateness or inappropriateness of accepting the word nigger to describe them as a people; then that is absolute proof that the plans of the slave traders, slave breeders, and slave owners from centuries ago have come to fruition. Nowadays; niggers (cut) create their own backdoors.

Afrikans must begin to understand the fundamental and complicated mechanisms involved in the process of dehumanization. Afrikans must begin to acknowledge that it is a process which seeks out justifications to strip us of our humanity and our basic human rights, often through ersatz science, bogus religions and religious beliefs and social propaganda; to justify incarceration, occupation, extermination and annihilation.

(Chapter Seven)

"Black Dysfunctional Socialization"

Formerly, when you did not know God, you were slaves to those who by nature are not gods. But now that you know God, or rather are known by God, how is it that you are turning back to those weak and miserable principles? Do you wish to be enslaved by them all over again? You pay special attention to certain days, months seasons and years. I am worried about you. Can it be that all my work for you has been for nothing?

Galatians 4:8-11

It has frequently been said, *"With understanding comes knowledge."* This assemblage of essays is being written with the intention of bettering the lives and the quality of living of the many, which now exist under the yoke of oppression. These essays are being written in an endeavor to enhance understanding and to supply knowledge. Fact based enlightenment, with a foundation based on straightforward understanding and factual knowledge, is the key which will loosen the lock, which secures the shackles that incarcerate Black minds, and in turn imprisons Black bodies, and interns Black souls.

Unbeknownst to many, although the strings of Black oppression outwardly gives the impressions of being controlled by internal religious, social and political influences, within the control of Black communities; the reality of Afrikan oppression is that, it is in fact a designed oppression, which has been programmed to be a consequentially, continuous, effecting phenomenon which is premeditated to manipulate and control the conquered and surrendered mindsets, of the oppressed. In reality, the strings of Black oppression are in fact being manipulated by external religious, social, scientific and political influences outside the control of Black communities; often using and exploiting Black influential entities, to the detriment of Afrikan peoples.

Malevolent manipulations, and fraudulent exploitations are the oppressors' tools; and Black's acquiescent admissions of defeat, coupled with unclear, disingenuous ways of thinking, which subscribe to misleading preordained justifications which substantiate the Afrikan's incarceration are fast becoming reasonable and standardized, Black and societal predeterminations. Though, forces and influences outside of the Afrikan communities manipulate the strings, it's the Afrikans' obligation to sever these strings of manipulation and to take control over our own actions, whilst attaining the power to fashion, and manage our own destinies.

As dysfunction, and needless violence completely eviscerates the hearts and souls of impoverished Black communities, the people that dwell in these communities despondently languish in ambivalent, introverted existences, isolated by societal, political, and racial conditions, which stir up unsympathetic and indifferent responses from those both inside, and outside these communities. Disengaged from the larger functional society, and inundated by perceived dysfunctional moralities and principles which are erroneously labeled as *survivalists' tactics*; discouraged Black communities are completely marginalized, thoroughly victimized and absolutely demoralized! Faux cultural dysfunctions are being disguised to be virtuous Black cultures.

Under the spurious pretenses of community, and civil rights activism, defunct, exploitive, publicity seeking groups and individuals, now voraciously prey upon the grief stricken families and victims of violent crimes, and horrific homicides. Exploitation is their motivation, and without hesitation they enthusiastically exploit any and all situations to their advantage, despite the morbidity and the seriousness of the situations. They offer no reasons for, or any practicable solutions to, the deadly dilemmas now senselessly plaguing Black and impoverished communities. As numerous ineffectual, media created, community activists, march into Black communities exploiting the most overwhelming, and cataclysmic moments in any coherent person's life; catastrophic exploitation becomes the activists' occupations, which offers economic compensation for the parasitic "community" activists, while contributing no reasons for, or answers to, the deadly dilemmas, which daily plague and devastate the distraught victims, or their besieged and distressed communities.

Many local and national groups and individuals fundamentally function to exploit the oppressed victims of disheartened and disoriented communities, by parasitically highlighting the problems of the victimized, for the attainment of fame and fortune; which allows the exploitation of Black communities by its' oppressors.

Outwardly, many groups and community activists may give the impressions that their hearts are in a good place. Yet, in truth, many are looking for fame, fortune, validation and adulation from the media, and both the dominant society and the oppressed victims; all the while, the desperate, devastated exploited victims continually suffer, sinking deeper and deeper into the depths of depression, despair, and hopelessness.

Inwardly, the ineptness of the phony community activists are actually likened to placebos; psychologically soothing psyches and situations, while in reality contributing no remedying effects. Consequently; people exploited by the self-centered exploitations of these parasitic leaders, keep dying, slow, agonizing deaths.

Unconscious Thoughts and Consequences

Unfortunately and unconsciously, many look into our communities and look at our people and see mental illness as the problem which overwhelmingly affects our people. Regrettably, they don't see that much of what they view as mental illness, can in actually be attributed to a deliberate, "dysfunctional socialization." Afrikans were consciously made into slaves and unconsciously we still function with a slave's psychology.

Granted while mental illness is a widespread problem in Black communities, dysfunctional socialization is a more rampant problem amongst Black people in Black communities. Unconsciously (without conscious thought), Black people subscribe to irrational and oftentimes dysfunctional trends, behaviors and cultures without ever giving it a second thought. They subscribe to diets designed to kill them, religions; which by design diminish and oppress them, and cultural trends; which by design, dehumanize and murder them!

Conscious Thoughts & Conscious Actions

The capacity for any people to remove the constraints of their oppression and manage their own destinies resides within each individual, and can be made possible, by initiating courageous **acts** of consciousness. Conscious thought without conscious actions in reality should be characterized as, unproductive states of unconsciousness or semi-consciousness. Conscious thought in conjunction with courageously conscious actions, embolden people with the authority, and the abilities to confront their oppressors, seize control of their lives, and establish their own destinies. Conscious thoughts provide the map and our actions free us.

Conscious thinking makes it possible for discouraged and subjugated people to recognize when there are disadvantageous campaigns of propaganda, being executed in confrontation to them. Conscious thinking devoid of conscious actions will allow dangerously disadvantageous curriculums of propaganda to persist unchallenged against the group, and eventually break through the straightforwardness of a group's reality with the dysfunctional falsehoods being premeditatedly created for the purposes of completely controlling, and destroying the people of the oppressed group, on every existential level.

Mentally, physically and spiritually; the conquered peoples' realities are totally marginalized, detrimentally fashioned and disadvantageously manipulated to the detriment of the group. It is for these exact reasons, that the conscious thinking people of every group have an obligation to consciously act on the behalf of all the people of the group. The conscious thinking people are those who have been bestowed with a Divine gift, and have a Divine obligation to think and act on behalf of, and in the best interests of all of the people.

Conscious thoughts with no conscious actions are in truth, spinelessly treacherous, and duplicitous deeds. Duplicitous deeds and spineless inactivity are ultimately recognized and acknowledged by the oppressors of Black people, and those Black apprehensions are then manipulated to the advantage of the oppressors of Black people. The oppressors' manipulations of conscious thinking Black peoples' apathetic indolence transforms conscious people, into naive collaborators, which unsuspectingly and unintentionally surrender to the disingenuous campaigns of the bigoted, as they ignorantly align themselves with those hell-bent on the destruction of our conscious Afrikan thoughts, conscious Afrikan actions, and every conscious Afrikan.

Tupac Shakur is one such duplicitous warrior often offering positive thoughts to entice the young followed by treacherously egregious acts of violence and treason which led and lead so many to their deaths, and continuously contributes to both the demolition of our communities, and to the destruction of our people.

Black Societal Backwardness

> *When you enter the land the Lord your God is giving you, do not learn to imitate the abominations of the nations there. Let no one be found among you who sacrifices his son or daughter in the fire, who practices divination or sorcery, interprets omens, engages in witchcraft, or casts spells, or who is a medium or spiritualist or who consults the dead.*
>
> *Anyone who does these things is an abomination to the Lord, and because of these abominations, the Lord your God will drive out those nations before you. Thou shalt be perfect with The Lord Thy God.*
>
> *Deuteronomy 18:9*

Societal backwardness; is by and large, characterized by Black peoples' powerlessness to determine and develop the appropriate societal competencies, to function productively within the larger society. Societal backwardness is often represented by, dysfunctional performance levels among Black people, which give both credibility and authenticity to the notion of White supremacy and racism, which traps Black people in the muck and mire of a premeditated; perceived need for Caucasian dependency, dysfunctional behavior, promiscuity, shameless ignorance, and a perceived cultural propensity for acts of criminality.

Regrettably, Black people have unresponsively inherited the complicated and problematically demanding responsibility (assignment) to eradicate from themselves, those disadvantageous occurrences of societal backwardness, and the predatory behaviors towards each other, before they can require White people to do the same. Interpreting The Bible, *"We must remove the logs from our own eyes before we can remove can remove the splinters from the eyes of our oppressors."* We must first and foremost correct ourselves!

Black people have to first methodically face up to, and dismantle their own, individual and unconstructive, dysfunctional demons of excessiveness, indifference, criminality, imprisonment, social unconsciousness, paranoia, promiscuity and cultural awareness; just to begin. Black people must begin to help themselves, by systematically developing, and utilizing the abilities that lay within each of us, to construct better lives for ourselves, our families, our communities, and our people. James Allen, author of the book, *As a Man Thinketh* once wrote, *"Thought is the seed, and action is the fruit which it bears."*

The 'educated Negroes' have the attitude of contempt toward their own people because in their own as well in their mixed schools, Negroes are taught to admire the Hebrew, the Greek, the Latin, and the Teuton and to despise the African...

Dr. Carter G. Woodson

Deep within the consciousnesses' of those African people who have surrendered to the archetypes of the racists, and now inconspicuously subscribe to their detrimental viewpoints, and defeated ways of thinking, surreptitiously indoctrinated into them by their oppressors; are fundamentally damaging obsessions, to lift up their oppressors to the expertly qualified positions of scientific specialists, divine authorities, behavioral educators, and those people worthy of adulation, admiration and exaltation. Psychologically speaking, an overwhelming majority of Black people endure the clinically coined, psychological condition articulated as "Stockholm Syndrome." They have unquestionably and absolutely; fell in love with their conquerors.

'Stockholm Syndrome' *is a psychological reaction often demonstrated by kidnapped hostages, in which the hostages demonstrate signs of "love and loyalty" to their hostage-takers, regardless the objectionable consequences, the dangers or the risks to the hostages. This syndrome was named following a robbery in Stockholm, Sweden, in which bank robbers held bank employees as their hostages from August 23 to August 28 in 1972. (The hostages protected them and two of the hostages later married the two hostage-takers.)*

On that occurrence, the hostages became psychologically and emotionally attached to the hostage-takers and even safeguarded their captors after they were freed from their six day ordeal. Their misfortune only lasted six days. Now try to imagine to what measures, and to what levels, these psychological conditions must be affecting on the once enslaved, imprisoned and oppressed psyches of Afrikan people in America and the world over, after centuries of incarceration, subjugation and domination. Try to imagine six days of confinement in comparison to six barbaric centuries of dehumanizing chattel enslavement.

At this time, Afrikan peoples are being disadvantageously acculturated to the detriment of themselves, by way of counterfeit programs of assimilation, which are by design, intended to make African people evolve into a dysfunctional race of people. From the moment they wake in the morning, until the second they fall to sleep at night, Afrikan children and young Afrikan adults particularly, are the premeditated objectives of racially provoked programs of propaganda, fashioned to negatively socialize Afrikan people as a group; to appear to be intrinsically dysfunctional, and to be understandingly accepted, as the socially dysfunctional buffoons and criminals that God created us, and then cursed us (Black) to be. We are being programmed to be both dysfunctional and inferior by the dominant culture of this society, for the benefit of the bigots.

Occupational forces which operate from outside Black communities, whose theaters of operation, function from the heart of our communities, are indeed influencing, manipulating and uncompromisingly controlling the dysfunctional socialization processes, calculated for the underdevelopment, the extermination and the premeditated incarceration of Black people, for the intensification and preservation of White supremacy.

The foremost objective of all White Supremacists is to preserve White supremacy at any and all costs! In their eyes; White supremacy is the safe-guard which insures the existence of the White race, and insures that White people will always be the dominant, governing body, which controls all other races of peoples.

It has long been a strategy and a practice for outside forces to reward behaviors, which both demonstrate and contribute to the destructive and disadvantageous dealings, which tear down Black people and Black communities, while simultaneously penalizing, and reprimanding the constructive behaviors and attitudes, which have proved to be advantageous and even heroic for, and amongst Afrikan people (Judas Iscariot).

Productive acts and actions, within Black communities, which have proved to be advantageous for Afrikan people whilst at the same time proving to be threatening to White supremacy; are customarily defined and viewed pessimistically by the bigots as being racially antagonistic, militant, and unpatriotic. The bigots set the parameters for the characterizations, which frequently, negatively characterize the oppressed people. Unfortunately, the demoralized, exploited victims very frequently; eagerly concede to the unsubstantiated, disadvantageous and illogical characterizations, which are often created to control, discredit, and destroy Afrikans, and their heroic and honorable champions. Their malicious campaign of propaganda is working.

Controlled Thought

> *"If you can control a man's thinking, you don't have to worry about his actions. If you can determine what a man thinks you do not have worry about what he will do. If you can make a man believe that he is inferior, you don't have to compel him to seek an inferior status, he will do so without being told and if you can make a man believe that he is justly an outcast, you don't have to order him to the back door, he will go to the back door on his own and if there is no back door, the very nature of the man will demand that you build one."*
>
> *Dr. Carter G. Woodson*

Regrettably, the oppressors of Black people constantly keep Black people disorientated, divided amongst each other and completely alienated from the world. The oppressors of Black people kidnapped a people who are fundamentally a socialist people; perverted socialism into a profanity, eduKKKated Africans to be socially dysfunctional and forced Afrikans to be in opposition to their basic temperaments; surrendering to narcissistic, capitalistic and materialistic ideologies, which are coupled with racially motivated, xenophobic approaches. The racists' malicious psychological reprogramming misinforms and confuses not only Black people, but the whole of humankind. Psychological programming makes Blacks appear less than human.

The racially motivated, premeditated manipulations of cultural misinterpretations, has compelled the world and particularly Black people, to function within dangerously misinformed ways of thinking, and to employ disadvantageously manipulated psychological approaches. Unfounded acknowledgements of unscientific fabrications, acceptances of noticeable falsehoods as authenticities, and submitting to counterfeit cultures and fictitious sciences are some of the tools and techniques implemented by the racists to maintain power over our realities, and are the crucial evidences of racially motivated and contrived thought manipulations.

The promoters, supporters, and benefactors (those who gain advantages) of White supremacy, by means of deceitful manipulations of psychological dysfunctions, societal influences, and the absolute unmitigated control over all informational and media outlets; they continuously make bigoted attempts to redefine, and reconstruct the Afrikan's history, the Afrikan's psyches and all Afrikan people. Fraudulent reconstructions of history and counterfeit remanufactures of cultures coupled with forged manipulations of Afrikan images, and normality's, become powerfully effective ways of manipulating Afrikan, and global thought processes.

Collectively, Afrikan people have been so completely conquered, so thoroughly divided, and so absolutely socialized dysfunctional; and our xenophobia has grown to be so extreme, that we have irrationally turned our fear of strangers inwardly towards our Afrikan selves. Afrikans' lack of self-knowledge, have made us strangers to ourselves; and Afrikan levels of self-hatred are disgracefully, and historically unprecedented.

"Know Thyself."

Ancient Greek Aphorism

Long before the advent of chattel slavery, the Afrikans' oppressors forbid Afrikans knowledge of self, even to the point of eradicating and re-creating Afrikan history. The racists made Afrikans strangers, even unto themselves. Never before, in any of the unbounded interpretations of this planet's illustrious history, have any people hated themselves more than Black people! How coherent is it for any people, to display more allegiance to, and to have more kindness towards their oppressors, than they do for their own reflections?

The Afrikans' reflections, daily witnessed in our very own mirrors now instigate self-loathing within Afrikan people. When did our wide noses, our thick lips, our curly hair, and our dark skin, become so gruesomely unattractive? The racists' eduKKKations demand that we view ourselves, and be viewed by the world, as objectionably unattractive, less intelligent and absolutely a lesser human; to be disrespected by the world.

Behavioral Modification (Positive Reinforcement)

Initially, the Caucasian enslavers of Afrikan people assumed that their brutal disciplining, and unemotional punishment of their Afrikan slaves were the best techniques to accomplish control of their slaves, manage their behavior (train them), and to make the Afrikan slaves more productive for their owners. Increasingly, the Caucasian slave owners began to consciously recognize, that positive reinforcement techniques were far superior to their preceding methods of merciless punishment, and ruthless reprimands.

It was long ago understood and acknowledged that, positive reinforcement was more effectively beneficial than the brutal discipline and resulted in long-lasting behavioral modifications, whereas harsh punishment only momentarily altered slave behaviors; presenting numerous disadvantages, and injurious side effects.

Punishments provoked injuries, deaths, resentments, detestation, and insurgences in opposition to many of the slave owners. Alternatively; positive reinforcements used together with effective manipulation both compensated and encouraged the continuation of desired slave behaviors; even though those behaviors proved to be detrimental to the individual slaves, and disadvantageous their groups. Evidently, individual comforts amongst the slaves, apparently outweighed any group concerns, no matter how momentary.

Punishment is not just the opposite of positive reinforcement. When it pertains to behavioral modification and alteration, it has been scientifically proven and established, that methods which employ techniques of positive reinforcement, are likely to be more advantageous, than methods utilizing sadistic punishment. It is very important that we gain a full understanding of this process so that we can fight against this process and absolutely invalidate the affects of these practices, for the fortification and enrichment of our people.

Afrikans must eliminate from within themselves the iniquitous modes of thinking which both summons and gives permission to those destructive forces determined to destroy Afrikan people. Prejudiced Caucasian oppressors control, sanction, condemn and disseminate damaging nigga imagery throughout every Black neighborhood, and the world. Many presume that Black people have no control over the negative images of Black people, which White people, put on exhibit, and broadcast throughout our communities, America, and the world. Furthermore, countless numbers of us do not believe that the negative images of us are in any way disadvantageous or detrimental to us as a people. Quote, *"A picture is worth a thousand words."*

Therefore, there are those within our communities who have surrendered to the trickery, subscribed to the buffoonery, and genuinely believe, that those destructively dysfunctional performances and images are in actuality rebelliously defiant, and courageously honorable acts and characterizations. Unconsciously and without thinking many Black people routinely cash counterfeit cultural checks for which many will sell their souls, sell out their people, and mortgage their futures. Whenever a mistreated group sits silently as their enemies negatively wholesale unconstructive images of them to the world, it is equated to participating in silent auctions; where unconcerned silence, unconsciously seals tremendously treacherous transactions, as once again, apathetically comatose Afrikan souls are grimly placed and sold upon the auction blocks.

"If you can't convince them, confuse them."

President Harry S. Truman

The terminologies positive reinforcement, and negative reinforcement, absolutely undertakes entirely new characterizations when they are appropriately associated with Afrikan peoples. The adversaries of Black people have cagily distorted the game by perplexing Black peoples' collective equilibriums and upsetting Afrikan peoples' true comprehensions of right and wrong; flipping Afrikan consciousnesses' upside down and inside out. Consequently, their positive reinforcements; *"rewarding of negative behaviors"* are in truth negative reinforcements, and their negative reinforcements; *"punishing positive behaviors"* are in actuality also negative (destructive) reinforcements. We must forever remember that, two negatives are a double negative, and double negatives never make a positive. *"If you can't convince them, confuse them."*

Eventually, we realize that we are functioning from within distorted realities and perverted systems based in confusing double negatives, which in reality turn out to be racially contrived negatives, which advances the bigoted interests of the Caucasian oppressors, and positively (absolutely), protects White supremacy. The distorted realities and systems, from which Afrikans now function, are premeditated to strengthen the perverted dysfunctions from which many Afrikans operate. Spurious psychosomatic systems designed to unconstructively influence, and manipulate Afrikan people's religious, social, psychological and economic realities, have been premeditatedly introduced into Afrikan communities, in customs, which are by design; intended to look like constructive actions, whilst simultaneously, underhandedly stimulating, dysfunctional cultures and creating unconstructive results. These *"established (or ritualized)"* surreptitiously, calculated systems of dysfunction, shall be called, *"Dysfunctional Fortifiers."*

Dysfunctional Fortifiers

"Dysfunctional Fortifiers" are meticulously designed, disadvantageous systems, and institutions, which are crafted to bear resemblances to constructively encouraging traditional institutions of empowerment, whilst at the same time, producing negative, damaging, unproductive and ineffective results. These systems of dysfunctional fortification are designed, manufactured and established by our oppressors, to continuously encourage, and reinforce inadequate performances, unconstructive behaviors, apathetic approaches and counterfeit systems of belief. These fortifiers are commonly designed to be self sustaining systems, and more importantly, they are knowingly calculated to seem as inherently negative, self-fulfilling prophesiers.

In these closing paragraphs, I will attempt to concisely identify, define, and examine a few of the systemic dysfunctions which significantly affect us as a people. Unfortunately, the dysfunctions which detrimentally affect us a people are too numerous; continuously being fashioned, tweaked and fortified to reinforce the devastating clutch of dysfunction, which is being uncompromisingly implemented against Afrikan peoples.

Bigoted Caucasians fashioned the systems, corrupted Afrikan minds, created Black (Negro) mindsets and then positioned them as the automated mechanisms, which will automatically strengthen their racially and culturally oppressive systems. Moreover, niggers are the fruits' of their wickedly bigoted racial corruption. Racist Caucasians changed the Afrikans' way of thinking, and then distorted the Africans' values by first devaluing Africans' lives, dehumanizing African people, creating niggers and then increasing the niggers' covetous faith (voracious belief) in materialism. Starting with the parents of Black children; for centuries, xenophobic Caucasians have assaulted Black value systems, in endeavors to kill Afrikan children before they even have a chance to grow; making normal those dysfunctional behaviors, of dysfunctional people, by constantly rewarding their destructively dysfunctional activities and performances of nigger buffoonery.

With the introduction motion pictures, television, radio, the internet, and a plethora of other media outlets; wicked Caucasian oppressors have seized control of Afrikans' imagery, and apprehended psychological control of the Afrikans' mode of thinking. With this enormous amount of control, the oppressors recreate and control Afrikans' history, our contemporary presences, and determine our futures. With this unlimited amount of control, we permit them to define and redefine us; at a moments notice, and at a racist's whim.

In the next few paragraphs I will demonstrate the mechanism, bring to light the exploitative nature of the mechanism and demonstrate the disadvantageous consequences of a selected number of dysfunctional fortifiers. I will attempt to keep these passages brief, educational, constructive, pertinent, and truthful.

"Dysfunctional Black Parents"
(The Most Significant Dysfunctional Fortifiers)

As they grow up dysfunctional; could Black parents be the reason we are losing so many of our Children? As generations of vanquished Black children evolve into defeated adults, caught up in them dysfunctional situations of which they seemingly have no control; too few of us appear to truly be concerned about them and most assuredly far too few of us are providing the development and support that they need to mature, and avoid the overabundance of racist institutions, premeditatedly fashioned for the purpose of ensnaring, incapacitating, incarcerating, and annihilating our children. Those same dysfunctional people, created by their racist society, to the detriment of Afrikan people, are now charged with developing Afrikan children.

In reality, for too many, the very same people who are morally obligated to encourage and strengthen our children have instead themselves, grown into the very mechanisms utilized to constantly bring about their children's destruction, by underwriting their dysfunction. The premeditated cycle of dysfunctional children growing into dysfunctional parents, creating and raising more dysfunctional children to grow into still more dysfunctional parents, for the purpose of maintaining a permanent racial underclass, is continuous.

Not intending to insult, or assault Black families, Black parents or Black children, I do realize that some of these passages may give the impression of judgmental insensitivity. Nevertheless, in reality, these words are very much demonstrative of an exceedingly affectionate *"Souljah,"* uncompromisingly compassionate for his people, and the whole of humanity. Children are the most defenseless souls in society, and Black children are the most susceptible and the most defenseless souls in every segment of any society. When generational race based dysfunctions evolve into Black normality's; think of these passages as cold water being thrown into your faces, attempting to wake you up!

Cultureless; Black children grow to be culture whores; desperately clinging to the insignificant remnants of dysfunctional, racially skewed cultures, which demand and makes it possible for them to easily submit to the detrimentally contrived, counterfeit cultures of the culture vultures. Raised without the advantages of any legitimate culture, Black children confusingly gravitate to the counterfeit racial remnants of narrow-minded cultures which only allow them partial, and racially restricted memberships.

Disorientated; Unguided Black children, without direction, impulsively seek out role models (even though they be inappropriate) to correctly guide their steps, from adolescence to adulthood, as it is naturally done with all species inhabiting this planet. Unfortunately, as Afrikan children unconsciously embark upon their anticipated sojourns through life, their inherently instinctive journeys are malevolently ambushed by sinful, conscienceless people who encompass no passion or compassion for Black children. Subsequently, they place traps for children that confuse, incapacitate, eviscerate, and eventually incarcerate Afrikan children. And, the dysfunctional instructions of dysfunctional parents often aid in their incapacitation, incarceration and (character and physical) assassinations of their own children.

Neglected; Economically insufficient, and morally bankrupt Black Mothers, often vilify and crucify *several* adolescent and economically deficient Black Fathers; as scripted (preprogrammed) by those issuing their orders. Their personal trials, tribulations and confrontations evolve into preoccupations, which oftentimes confound parental judgments, responsibilities and obligations, and their ordained parental responsibilities, and obligations develop into the apathetic delegations of other people; and their children's educations and socialization become the sole (soul) occupations of the oppressors, and television and radio stations.

Meanwhile, jealous animosities disseminates detestation and loathing (hate) between the *several,* morally and economically bankrupt Black Fathers, and none of the *several* Black Fathers really respects, or loves any of the other Black Fathers, or the Mother of the children of the others; and certainly not those bastard children of (them other niggas) those other *"several"* Black Fathers!

"Dysfunctional Media Outlets"
(The Most Influential Dysfunctional Fortifiers: Television, Radio, Internet, Etcetera)

While many think that parents are the most influential components of their children's lives, unfortunately it has been proven that, the various media outlets (television, radio, internet, and etcetera) are in reality, the most influential facets of both the children's and the parents' lives. Many have said, "The television; is the most dangerous invention of the Twentieth Century!" And; regrettably, this too is confirmed to be true!

The various media outlets, and especially television, have become societal shapers, cultural initiators and educational fortifiers. They have become our parents, teachers and baby-sitters. Their media; instills our values, inculcates our ideologies, encourages our morality, and indoctrinates our spirituality. Parents and their children are incessantly being thrust into calculatingly, premeditated systems of indoctrination, which are designed to bring about a desired process of socialization; be it functional or dysfunctional.

Unfortunately, for Afrikan people, our oppressors control the media and in turn control the mechanisms of our realities. The xenophobic oppressors of Afrikan people initiate our cultures, manage our edukkkation, inculcate our ideologies, instill our values, encourage our morality and indoctrinate our spirituality. Racist people design Black peoples' realities, create Black personalities and dictate Blacks' spirituality. Behavior proved to be dysfunctional and detrimental to Afrikan people, are most frequently encouraged, celebrated and rewarded by those racially discriminatory people that are in command of the media, which formulates and fashions Afrikan realities.

Dysfunctional images, which unsympathetically stereotypes Black people, are broadcast around the world as cultural normality's for Black people, with the twofold intention of;

(1) Falsely edukkkating Afrikans and the world as to the Afrikans' true and inherent nature and;

(2) Socializing Afrikan people and the world to believe that Afrikans are a (God cursed) self-prophesized, self-destructive and naturally dysfunctional race of degenerate beings with unnatural inclinations towards criminality, and immorality.

"Black Churches/ Religious Dysfunctions"
(The Spiritually Influential Dysfunctional Fortifier)

More often, led by dysfunctional Black preachers, Black churches are the most significantly dysfunctional spiritual fortifiers, which will forever insure that Black people will forever function in the role to the vassals, in the racists' oppressively controlled societies. Pimping, pimped out, self-proclaimed protagonist of God and God's words; the Bible warns us, *"By their fruits ye shall know them."* Emulating, and impersonating pimps, these arrogant servants of God instruct their flocks to exist as sheep, as they themselves don the clothing of ravenous wolves, incessantly and parasitically, devouring and gorging at the expense of their of their impoverished and spiritually bankrupt flocks; as they lie dead and dying in impoverished pastures.

Black preachers preach about the flock, preach down to the flock, and preach at the flock; never speaking to the flock for the emboldening of the flock, whilst simultaneously fleecing them for Caesar's thirty pieces of silver. Just like Judas Iscariot, leading the Romans to Jesus, Black preachers continually acknowledge the destructive images created by the enemies of our youth, and then exploit those very same images, for the thirty pieces of silver offered up by our oppressors. Dysfunctional and devastatingly damaging images of our youth, become racist commodities, to be bought and sold, to the disadvantage of us all.

It is insane for conquered people put their problems in the hands of their oppressors. Nevertheless, Black people tend to place their problems in the hands of imaginary deities produced especially for them, by the very same people which enslaved them. They tend to place their problems, not only in the hands of their oppressors' but, into the make-believe hands, of them make-believe gods which despise and abhor them. Most often, those dysfunctions which are depicted in the media and broadcast by the media are *"Divinely"* legitimized in the pulpit, and become self actualized (prophesized) dysfunctions.

Pimping, pimped out, self-proclaimed protagonists of God's word, the Bible warns us, "By their fruits ye shall know them." They imitate pimps and they are not the humble servants of God as instructed; ye shall know them by their fruits, and their fruits are those reminiscent of pimps.

Conclusion

Dysfunctional Socialization is at the root of the majority of our problems as Afrikan people in America, and unfortunately, Black people in America are being drowned by this dilemma. Completely engulfed, and so thoroughly inundated by this phenomenon, that for many of us, we cannot see the forest for the trees.

Submerged, and encased in the pollution of dysfunctions, many now wrongly recognize dysfunction as an environment of normality. When children grow up existing in realities found on those fallacies established for them by our oppressors; the forged cultural dysfunctions of their oppressors, from which they exist, will unquestionably become their realities.

Creating Conducive Environments

Parents are on the front lines and bear the brunt of the responsibility, for creating environments conducive to the upbringing, uplifting and enrichment of their children. If the truth be told, every parent is duty-bound to construct and control the environments, conducive to their children. It is important that parents begin to understand, that it is not only what is to be expected of them but, it is an indispensable responsibility, that each parent be responsible for the creation, and the supervision of advantageously positive environments, which will continuously promote safety, positive behaviors and rehabilitative qualities.

As we develop into adults, those same conscientiousness parental responsibilities become our social and civic responsibility, and the moral obligation of all adults.

The Afrikan struggle is a struggle which more frequently finds its point of emanation beginning from within various Black communities. Black people often choose to see only the perceived good and refuse to see the dysfunctional, negative, and more often than not, sanctioned criminal activities of many of those in our Black communities.

Community Empowerment

Objectively, step back; stepping outside of yourselves, and your communities, for just a moment, and look back in, at the communities from which Afrikans exist. Objectively look at all of the groups, organizations, institutions and associations which allege to be fighting for the development and empowerment of Afrikan people. Almost everyday, we hear the impassioned cry of, "We have to come together, and stand united, as a people!" Would someone please tell me, "How do we come together and stand together as a people united, when so many of these individualistic groups, organizations, institutions, and individuals, are even struggling against one another, and within themselves?" Why do so many of us seem to, enthusiastically bestow so much power and respect to those most dysfunctional and disadvantageous to our communities and to us as a people? Black people have historically heaped praise and adulation on societal criminals.

Dysfunctional Socialization (also acknowledged, and recognized as *Societal Backwardness*), is frequently characterized by a peoples' unmitigated powerlessness to determine and develop the appropriate societal competencies, which make it possible for them to function successfully and realistically as a section of the whole of society. The realities of them, which are premeditatedly socialized to be dysfunctional, are often purposely distorted, and calculatingly fashioned, using established stereotypical programs of propaganda, which keeps them both subservient, and subordinate to the dominate culture. Dysfunctional Socialization is commonly characterized by disadvantageous unsatisfactory academic and societal performance levels, stereotypical propaganda-based cultures, and distinctively substandard societal structures, complete with inferior core value systems.

I now submit to you, this platter of *Soul Food* for thought; *Soul Food* to nourish and replenish the soul.

"The Sins of Their Fathers"

Thou shalt have no other gods before me.

Thou shalt not make unto thee any graven image, or any likeness of any thing that is in heaven above, or that is in the earth beneath, or that is in the waters under the earth:

Thou shalt not bow down thyself to them, nor serve them: for I the LORD thy God am a jealous God, visiting the iniquity of the fathers upon the children unto the third and fourth generation of them that hate me;

Exodus 20; 3-5

The sins of the fathers; often misguide the steps of their sons, subjecting future generations to damnation,
Programmed to fail; for many their rites of passage include sojourns through jail and lives of incarceration;
And, wicked imaginations encourage demeaning salutations, incarcerations and deviations of graduations,
While periods of intoxication and sexual gratification become more important than children's expectations!

Thou shalt have no other gods before me. Thou shalt not bow down thyself to them, nor serve them: for I the LORD thy God am a jealous God, visiting the iniquity of the fathers upon the children unto the third and fourth generation of them that hate me;

Exodus 20; 3/5

With the separation and elimination of spiritual foundations God and religion are just another machination,
And, monetary compensation, sexual contemplations, materialistic deliberations, and adoration/idolization;
Excitedly becomes their innermost and fundamental fascinations leading to devastation and incarceration,
As they engage in illegal activities and occupations due to their lack of education, and spiritual foundation!

Thou shalt have no other gods before me. Thou shalt not bow down thyself to them, nor serve them: for I the LORD thy God am a jealous God, visiting the iniquity of the fathers upon the children unto the third and fourth generation of them that hate me;

Exodus 20; 3/5

As many fathers *lie* under the yoke of incarceration; "Who is home making those fatherly determinations?"
When jails and prisons are filled to the brim, with the desolate souls of millions, of every racial persuasion;
Who is home for their celebrations of special occasions and the prevention of incarceration's devastation?
Your children get misdirected educations from television stations, and your absences become causations!

Thou shalt have no other gods before me. Thou shalt not bow down thyself to them, nor serve them: for I the LORD thy God am a jealous God, visiting the iniquity of the fathers upon the children unto the third and fourth generation of them that hate me;

Exodus 20; 3/5

They see hip fathers under the yoke of incarceration and their admiration leads to occupational emulation,
Yet, like Judas; street savvy fathers guard their reputations, their occupations, and betray family relations,
Indifferent to parental responsibilities and accountabilities; their foundations are situations of incarceration:
And, fathers become the causations for the perpetuation of devastation, and continuation of incarceration!

Thou shalt have no other gods before me. Thou shalt not make unto thee any graven image, or any likeness of any thing that is in heaven above, or that is in the earth beneath, or that is in the water under the earth: Thou shalt not bow down thyself to them, nor serve them: for I the LORD thy God am a jealous God, visiting the iniquity of the fathers upon the children unto the third and fourth generation of them that hate me;

Exodus 20; 3-5

"Mustafa Rasul Al-Amin"
(Thursday, July 1, 2010)

"Judas' Thirty Pieces of Silver"
(The Judas Goats)

Following Judas, and Judas' lead; young brothers and sisters ignorantly line up to sell their souls,
Like Judas Goats, dismal role models, deadly trends, and destructive fashions lead to grim goals,
And, thirty pieces of silver, becomes the actors' motivations, to act out deadly conspiratorial roles,
And, many allow dysfunction, destruction, and death into our abodes, disguised as cultural molds!

Yesterday; I walked in the presence of dream-filled children filled with hopes, dreams and goals,
Today; out of fear I steer clear of baggy pants niggas, tight clothed hoes, and childish lost souls,
And, thirty pieces of silver becomes the actors' motivations to act out deadly conspiratorial roles,
And many allow dysfunction, destruction and death into our abodes, disguised as cultural molds!

For thirty pieces of silver they will sell their own, misleading Black folks hopes; like Judas Goats!

Hip-Hop's misogynistic overtones are causing young brothers, to lose respect for their mothers,
Hip-Hop's misogynistic overtones are causing their mothers, to lose respect for young brothers,
And thirty pieces of sliver become the actors' motivations to act out scenes produced by others,
As they encourage dysfunction, destruction, and death, aiding and abetting the plans of others!

Dysfunctional intellectual overtones are causing young sisters, to lose respect for their mothers,
Dysfunctional intellectual overtones are causing our mothers to lose respect for their daughters,
And thirty pieces of sliver become the actors' motivations to act out scenes produced by others,
As many encourage dysfunction, destruction and death, aiding and abetting the plans of others!

For thirty pieces of silver they will sell the pussy, misleading Black folks hopes; like Judas Goats!

Drug dealers' occupations become causations for admiration and emulation, of sick aspirations,
As many now out of frustration forsake traditional, legal occupations and permissible vocations,
And thirty pieces of silver are the actors' motivation to convince our children forsake education,
As without hesitation dysfunction, destruction and death are applauded with standing ovations!

And, as the glorification of criminal occupations, are met with joyful ovations, by the populations,
Criminal occupations, lead to the stereotypical criminalization of entirely subjugated populations,
And, thirty pieces of sliver becomes the actors' motivation, for the demoralization of populations,
As they encourage dysfunction, destruction, and death; aiding and abetting xenophobic nations!

For thirty pieces of silver they'll sell his dope, leading Black folks to slaughter; like Judas Goats!

Black preachers instruct Black people to be jubilant in their captivity and view God as Caucasian,
Praying the prayers that the prey pray, to the predators, as the predators prey on Afrikan nations,
And, thirty pieces of silver is now their motivations, for the exploitation; of Afrikans to Caucasians,
As they promote them religious manipulations of Caucasians for monetarily religious occupations!

Preying on Black naivety, to gain financial security, in spite of White superiority and manipulation,
Monetary compensation become Judas' motivation, to secure Caucasian sponsored occupations,
And thirty pieces of silver becomes Judas' motivation, to lead Afrikans into Caucasian domination,
As they promote them religious manipulations of Caucasians for monetarily religious occupations!

For thirty pieces of silver, they trap and sell Black souls; leading Black folks, like the Judas Goats!
For thirty pieces of silver, they trap and sell Black souls; enslaving Black folks, like the Judas Goats!
For thirty pieces of silver, they trap and sell Black souls; slaughtering Black folks, like the Judas Goats!

"Mustafa Rasul Al-Amin"
(Sunday, November 9, 2008)

"SAGGIN"
(NIGGAS)

Inverse souls,
Stand before inversely reflecting mirrors,
Anguishing,
In various states,
Of,
Intentionally inflicted dyslexia,
And,
Inverted thoughts,
Produce inverse sight,
Standing,
In the mirrors,
NIGGAS,
See,
SAGGIN,
In the mirrors,
Whilst the mirrors truly reflect,
NIGGAS SAGGIN,
And,
SAGGIN NIGGAS ....

As,
Self-professed,
People of prosperity,
Lift up,
Inverted role models of notoriety,
Reflecting,
Destructive images of negativity,
Cloaked,
In illusionary images of productivity,
I,
Lift up,
Mirrors.......

Look into the mirror,
And reflect on this;
As *SAGGIN*,
Becomes the uniform of *NIGGAS*,
Is it by chance,
Or by design,
That *SAGGIN*,
Reflected in the mirror,
Spells *NIGGAS*?
And,
In the mirror's reflection,
Of *NIGGAS SAGGIN*,
Or *SAGGIN NIGGAS,*
Which is the illusion?
NIGGAS,
SAGGIN,
Or,
Both?

"Mustafa Rasul Al-Amin"
(Wednesday August 15, 2007)

"SAGGIN"
(NIGGAS)
(Part Two)

And,

Whilst self-professed NIGGAS,
Stand ignorantly SAGGIN;
Literally,
And figuratively,
Assed-out before all of humanity,
Professing SAGGIN to be,
The trendily voguish style of the contemporary NIGGAS,
And a fashionably undamaging act of youthful vanity,
As SAGGIN NIGGAS display their naivety,
By failing to distinguish the mirrored images,
Of,
NIGGAS and SAGGIN as a cloaked profanity,
Assuming a NIGGAS' celebrity is clothed in a SAGGIN vulgarity,
The NIGGAS' SAGGIN uniforms demonstrate their insanity!

The world bears witness,
As SAGGIN NIGGAS walk around with their pants pulled down,
And,
On many levels NIGGAS SAGGIN remind us of clowns,
Unconscious,
Black-faced clowns,
Walking around,
With pants pulled down,
In t-shirts pulled down like sexual night gowns,
Representative,
Of unconsciously sleep-walking SAGGIN NIGGAS,
In long,
Flowing, white night gowns,
With pants pulled way down,
And you make us ask,
Do conscious young Brothers,
And,
Mature men,
Walk around,
Like SAGGIN NIGGAS with their pants pulled down,
Like clowns?

NIGGAS forget, that Caucasians enslaved Afrikans and called them nigger to steal their humanity,
Fabricating and encouraging stereotypical behaviors of detriment, equating Afrikans with profanity,
Fashionably transforming their niggers into NIGGAS, and SAGGIN, is the uniform for their insanity,
And SAGGIN NIGGAS become braggart NIGGAS and un-informed uniformed symbols of insanity!
When did the evolutionary, revolutionary advancement of any people base its foundation in vanity?

SAGGIN NIGGAS refuse to understand, that those who named us nigger now encourage NIGGAS,
NIGGAS SAGGIN naively stand before metaphorically manipulated mirrors, thoughtlessly SAGGIN,
Thoughtlessly, unthinkingly thinking thoughtless thoughts without a thought, thoughtlessly NIGGAS,
Ostentatiously parade, thoughtlessly SAGGIN, in the debilitating uniforms, of un-informed NIGGAS!

"Mustafa Rasul Al-Amin"
(Monday, October 18, 2010)

"First Corinthian Chapter Thirteen Verse Eleven"

When I was a child; I spoke as a child, I understood as a child, I thought as a child: but when I became a man, I put away childish things.

King James Version

When I was a child;

I inherently possessed many child-like mannerisms and participated in many child-like activities,
I played childish games, dreamed impossible dreams, and regularly fantasized foolish fantasies,

I spoke as a child;

I childishly uttered the contemporary slang-filled languages to talk to children, and confuse men,
I spoke juvenile gibberish, encoded with concocted words intended to alienate men and women,

I understood as a child;

Unable to understand them simple, time tested lessons taught and learned by time and maturity,
Childish comprehensions complicates childish lives with rebellious futility aimed at any authority,

As a child I thought childish thoughts fraught with childish inaccuracies, and juvenile tendencies,
Juvenile tendencies which are oftentimes those delinquent tendencies that fills up penitentiaries,

At age eighteen many saw me as a man, but with no conscious awakening I never met the man,
Still speaking like a child with the understanding, and thinking of a child, "When will I be a man?"

When I was a child, I talked like a child; I reasoned like a child, I thought like a child.

When I became a man, I put childish ways behind me.

New International Version

Men: Talk to me about the things children do, and then talk to me about the things, that you do!
Men: Listen to conversations had by children, then listen to the conversations coming from you!
Men: Don't you understand that there are children depending you and on and looking up to you?
Men: You'll be a man when you stop thinking as a child and put those childish ways behind you!

"Great minds discuss ideas.
Average minds discuss events.
Small minds discuss people."

Eleanor Roosevelt

Mature minds entertain mature thoughts.....
When are you going to put those childish ways behind you?

"Mustafa Rasul Al-Amin"
(Saturday, August 28, 2010)

"When Did Dysfunction Become Debatable?"

Devious White media moguls create and authenticate, Black leaders to manipulate Black the fates,
Devilish media influences anoint, appoint and ordain White choices, and Black voices to enunciate,
Deviously using Black voices, and faces to obfuscate, complicate, explicate, and relate Black fates,
Dubiously pitting young and old, dysfunctional competitors on the world's stages in ersatz debates!

And White people have always.......

Created Black states and positioned Black leaders to manipulate, and oversee those Black states,
Recognizing the power of religion they exploited the pastor's gift of oration, to govern Black states,
Recognizing the power of music, they exploited a rappers' gift of oration to manipulate Black fates,
Even before the days of Willie Lynch, White's pitted sons against fathers, in dysfunctional debates!

And now.......

We watch as they validate and legitimate as leaders; community murderers with pending court dates,
And thugs and drug dealers sit on stages to participate in worldwide debates, that dictate Black fates,
Idiotic debates that legitimate and validate those idiotic words and behaviors, designed to incarcerate,
When did ideologies defensive of dysfunctional behaviors that daily incarcerate, become real debates?

And when we go to the grocery stores.......

We witness parents in the grocery stores, engaging in frenzied arguments with adolescent reprobates,
And we think, "Somebody needs to bust that baby's mother-fucking ass!" As their argument escalates!
Also we think, "The parents need to be kicked in the mother-fucking ass!" As their argument escalates!
When adults squabble with children, the children routinely make the adults look like foolish reprobates.

And I find it hard to believe.......

The arrogant preposterousness of camera-chasing Black leaders, participating in staged worldly debates,
With self-acknowledged thugs and drug dealers with criminal histories, warrants and pending court dates,
Normally dysfunctional behavior, warrants, and pending court dates would rightfully invalidate any debate,
Nevertheless, in frantic haste to validate debates, Black leaders haphazardly rush the stage to participate!

And seemingly, unbeknownst to them.......

Black leaders squander legitimate political opportunities, to participate on the world stage in fake debates,
Irresponsibly relinquishing the world stage to provide platforms for immature thugs and thieves to operate,
Cleverly utilizing Black voices and faces, to obfuscate, complicate, relate and wisely explicate Black fates,
Dubiously pitting young and old dysfunctional competitors on a world stage, to participate in faux debates!

So instead.......

The Black religious right engages those depraved Black criminals, in meaningless, dysfunctional debates,
As we witness our enemies' edukkkating our children, to participate in behaviors designed to exterminate,
And Black parents, unable to communicate descend to the depths of their children trying to communicate,
Fearing the backlash of those who create them they *lie* in unconcerned states too frightened to illuminate!

Not understanding that, they validate the reprobates; they rationally allow them to partake and participate,
Absurdly giving credibility to dysfunctional reprobates and meaningless debates as reprobates participate,
When did dysfunction become debatable, and why do so many of you; sanction reprobates to participate?

"Mustafa Rasul Al-Amin"
(Sunday October 28, 2007)

(Chapter Eight)

"Dysfunctional Hierarchy Of Black Social Structures"

"The Role Models That Black People Choose?"

The role models Black People "superficially" choose; make us appear so hypocritical,
Outwardly, Black people speechify about the heroes; who have been most beneficial,
Whilst, simultaneously opting to elevate and emulate; those people most detrimental,
They choose to ostracize those most spiritual; embracing the people most superficial,
As a People, we daily celebrate the spiritually eviscerated, and securely incarcerated,
Whilst continuously castigating the spiritually emancipated, and undeniably liberated!

"Mustafa Rasul Al-Amin"
(09042006)

Whilst still fresh on the subject of dysfunctional socialization, let us briefly examine the hierarchical social structures within Black communities. Remembering that, deliberately inflicted dysfunctions, were tools of the slave traders and are still the tools of racist's xenophobes. We must understand that our entire social structure has been compromised for the benefit and the empowerment of White supremacy.

Understanding this problem, it should not surprise anyone to know that Afrikans' social structures have for a fact, been deliberately created, and fashioned to be dysfunctional, in efforts to keep Afrikans dependent upon their Caucasian captors. The majority of us recognize on some existential level; something is out of whack when it comes to Black societal hierarchies. Conscious people can see the built in dysfunctions in Black societal hierarchies.

Inwardly, we all pretend to despise the criminal element in our communities. However, on the other hand; outwardly we honor, respect and celebrate criminals and criminal activity; frequently giving the impression of harboring deep fanatical fascinations and admiration for those unsociable, and pathological inclinations towards criminals, criminal activities, criminal thoughts, and immoral and unlawful acts. Dysfunctional and criminal mindsets, garner much more honor and admiration, than those hearts and souls with foundations in spirituality; within Black communities. For many of us, criminals are looked upon as rebellious heroes.

It is for this reason, that drug dealers operate openly, in virtual open air markets, and violently oppressive pimps in many cities openly, brutally and sadistically enslave women, oftentimes forcing them to be daily, and publicly raped, and then demand payment, for the raping, and the enslavement of them. It is for this reason that Black people and especially the Black youth, are being daily exposed to, and are being daily programmed by dysfunctional media sponsored programming, which "programs" Black minds to become discombobulated, and function normally, within dysfunctional psychological and sociological parameters.

The oppressors of Black people have psychologically programmed, and are programming Black people to accept and believe that, their dysfunctional mindsets, the dysfunctional behaviors in which, many willingly participate in, and those dysfunctional environments which many daily exist in; are common and inherent psychological traits and characterizations instilled within them as part of their evolutionary process. Many fail to understand that these dysfunctional traits are in reality programmed into them by fearful xenophobic slave traders and abhorrently racist bigots. Ersatz science and oppressive religions are the reinforcement mechanisms utilized by them to keep Afrikans under the inescapable yoke of oppression.

They have created gods in their image, and religious systems which encourage and protect their cultures; and now they sell them to you, as you once again, make your enslavement profitable, financing your own captivity. Churches and liquor stores on nearly every corner; insure an abundance of niggers in jail cells.

Basically, there are five major areas of concern when it pertains to the hierarchy of Black social structure:

(1) Dysfunctional Parents
(2) Dysfunctional Role Models
(3) Dysfunctional Addictions
(4) Dysfunctional Religions
(5) Dysfunctional Cultures (Incarceration And Criminality)

Dysfunctional Parents

When you think about it, it is absolutely criminal, the activities, and the programs, being imposed upon the impressionable young minds of Afrikan children. Physical and psychological assaults upon Black children are instigated in the womb, intensify during their formative years, and are totally reinforced throughout the balance of their racially predetermined life expectancies. Ironically, these unconscionable assaults on the minds, bodies and souls of Afrikan children are often permitted, with the blessings of Black parents; those same Black parents which are charged with the divine responsibility of growing their children in the divine light of *The Almighty Creator* of all things.

From inside the wombs of their mothers, many Black fetuses are poisoned by toxic atmospheres, noxious greasy diets, lethal doses of alcohol and drugs, and are extremely deficient in physiological, psychological and sociological encouragements. Many impoverished, Black mothers exist within stressful environments which are incorporated into and manifest within the development, and underdevelopment of their children.

During their adolescence and formative years, Afrikan children are incessantly fed unhealthy, nutritionally deficient diets, which contribute to their psychological, physiological, and evolutionary underdevelopment. Coupled with media endorsed psychologically dysfunctional diets of violence, sex, and the glorification of pathologically antisocial behaviors, children's minds are being fundamentally murdered even before they have a chance to grow; as Black parents are increasingly allowing these assaults on their children.

Consequently, as many Black people continue their sojourn through the trek of life; they journey through this life like robotic zombies, programmed to function dysfunctional, like second class citizens, who have outlived their usefulness to White supremacy; and with no contributions to the Black community, they are essentially waiting to die, whilst increasingly becoming burdens to, and upon the Black community.

Parents are the foundations of all civilizations charged with the mental, spiritual and physical cultivation of our most precious creations. Divine association coupled with the utilization of functional socialization and educations based upon foundations of realization are the crucial occupations of parents of all civilizations. However, parental preoccupation with criminalization and incarceration leads to a disassociation with our spiritual, educational and parental foundations, which in turn bring about dysfunctional socializations that lead to the machinations which insure our children's further incarceration and continuous devastation.

Dysfunctional Role Models

Since before I can first remember; them most celebrated and respected in Black communities are the very same people who are the most destructive to Black communities. These criminals' flamboyant styles and ill-gotten acquisitions, often overshadows, suffocates, and extinguishes the issues of honor, honesty, and integrity; and the superficiality of criminality becomes a Black normality and a pseudo Black reality. When entire communities stand indulgent of immoral acts and unlawful activities, and enthusiastically supportive of criminals, crimes and criminal behavior; criminals become virtuously idolized, heroic role models.

Everyone, from pompous pimps to pretentious preachers; their possessions seem to make palatable their iniquitous sins and increases their popularity and prosperity. Whilst honest, hardworking men and women working minimum wage jobs are often ridiculed and admonished as being weak and inferior. Whilst at the same time, those that prove to be most disadvantageous and most damaging to Afrikan people and Black communities are undoubtedly the most celebrated, the most emulated and the most venerated.

"Black Role Models"

As a People, we seem to celebrate the spiritually eviscerated, and securely incarcerated,
And, we apparently, tend to castigate the spiritually emancipated, and truthfully liberated,
And, people idolize of braggarts who sing praises of abusing hemp and emulating pimps,
And, people emulate, and elevate faux gangstas, who use and abuse women like wimps,
With animal-like mindsets their attractions to shiny objects are similar to those of chimps,
And, we learn, the hardest gangstas are sexually attracted to "men," whose wrist go limp,
As they promulgate, disseminate, and propagate all those people most disadvantageous,
And, denigrate, castigate, and eliminate those who have been proven, most courageous!

And I digress as Black Folk regress.......

"Mustafa Rasul Al-Amin"
(Monday June 12, 2006)

"The Role Models That Black People Choose?"

The role models Black People "superficially" choose; make us appear so hypocritical,
Outwardly, Black people speechify about the heroes; who have been most beneficial,
Whilst, simultaneously opting to elevate and emulate; those people most detrimental,
They choose to ostracize those most spiritual; embracing the people most superficial,
As a People, we daily celebrate the spiritually eviscerated, and securely incarcerated,
Whilst continuously castigating the spiritually emancipated, and undeniably liberated!

"Mustafa Rasul Al-Amin"
(09042006)

"Habitual Rituals"
(Black Murders)

The murdering of young Black men in AmeriKKKa, is recognized as predictable, habitual rituals,
Acceptable habitual rituals rooted in predictable, dysfunctional behaviors thought to be cultural,
Acceptable habitual rituals, rooted in predictable, dysfunctional behaviors taught to be cultural,
Untruthful, dysfunctional behaviors deliberately taught as cultural rituals, to affect the youthful!

"Mustafa Rasul Al-Amin"
(Tuesday September 30, 2008)

"The System"

Everyday.......

I watch as young people continuously get trapped in the system,
And evolve, into the disposable reprobates caught up in the system,
Foolishly becoming the apathetic fools, which daily try to play the system,
Ignorantly growing into the old men that become intricate parts of the system,
Ignorant, old men who are in reality, played by the system to justify the system!

"Mustafa Rasul Al-Amin"
(Wednesday, March 17, 2008)

Dysfunctional Addictions

No addiction is a good addiction. However, when I speak of dysfunctional addictions I am fundamentally speaking to those types of, *institutionalized addictions* that *idiosyncratically* influence Black communities.

Drugs and alcohol devastate Black communities in ways only comparable to those early Native American communities. We continuously hear the cliché, "A liquor store on every corner." However, nobody heeds this ominous warning, and it continuously falls upon deaf ears. In lieu of being acknowledged as plagues in Black communities, drugs and alcohol instead become viable sources of income, lucrative businesses; and the *procurators* of these morally wrong and often illicit operations become respected and admired for their devastating contributions to Black communities. Selling drugs becomes a commendable occupation.

In far too many families, drugs, alcohol and the illicit livelihood and lifestyle of selling them are frequently tolerated, promoted, encouraged and supported by parents, and family members. In many instances we witness generations of addicted families; whose addictions are so commonplace that we fail to recognize the symptoms or the dysfunction of their addictions. Instead many excuse, and find justifications for their weekly and oftentimes daily dysfunction by disguising them as sociable and family gatherings, condoning unlawful activities and encouraging and supporting criminals in their criminal endeavors.

Oftentimes, drug and alcohol addictions within addicted families begin with children as young as seven or eight years of age. Frequently juvenile and immature parents find humor in getting their children high and many see nothing wrong with using illegal drugs and alcohol around children. In numerous families, drug usage is so common that many children don't realize that it is an illegal activity; and as they grow up they become even more tolerant of, and desensitized to the illegal attributes of the drug and alcohol culture.

For each subsequent generation, the dysfunctional aspects of drugs and alcohol become less noticeable, as the dysfunction becomes more accepted as a generational and family normality. Eventually, the illicit acts of hustling and drug dealing soon become family-oriented enterprises, which everyone takes pride in. Consequently, each of these crime families become permanent members of an infamous underclass that forfeits many of their productive and formative years to incarceration, and to the fortification of the prison industrial complex.

Dysfunctional Religions

When Afrikan people surrender to religions, were the overriding images of that religion are predominantly of their oppressors and the images of them are scorned, that in itself is a dysfunction. When they submit to theologies which cast them in the roles of the accursed scoundrels of those theologies, cursed by their deities; then these are religions and theologies, which have been proved to be dysfunctional for Afrikans.

Religious teachers mockingly resembling pimps in stature and thought; like Judas Goats, they lead flocks of gullible sheep into slaughter in efforts to acquire their thirty pieces of silver. In Black communities, the most successful (prosperous) churches are those which acquire the greatest financial rewards. Spiritual salvation, redemption and reclamation are of little importance when one truly examines the functions and purposes of Black churches. As these churches convince people to tithe (give) ten, fifteen or twenty plus percent of their earnings, I must ask, "Where is the logic in giving away your hard earned earnings?" Do we now purchase blessings from God and the church? Furthermore, if we have no money do we receive no blessings?

"Afrikan Pathology"

The Christ mythology,
A Caucasian theology,
A Negro morphology,
This is the Afrikan's pathology!

"Mustafa Rasul Al-Amin"
(101101)

Dysfunctional Cultures

Since the time before Afrikans were first enslaved, bigoted programs had been initiated, and instituted for the purposes removing and replacing Afrikans' cultures with falsified, fabricated cultures created by those whose plan all along, was to subjugate and enslave Afrikans. Those racists that enslaved Afrikan people, systematically tricked Afrikans into questioning Afrikan cultures, convinced them to reject Afrikan cultures, and ultimately; after enslaving Afrikans, they forbid Afrikans to teach, speak about or even remember their cultures.

After attempting to completely destroy Afrikans' cultures, the next step of the racists plan was to instigate counterfeit, fabricated cultures in which they could manipulate to control the Afrikans mind, body and soul. So, they created slave culture, Jim Crow culture, Colored People's cultures, Negro culture, nigger culture, hip-hop culture and nigga culture. When a people forget their pasts; they are doomed to repeat them and culture is the shaper of our past, present and futures.

"The Assassination, Restoration And Coronation Of Flava Flav"
(Long Live The King Of The Clowns)

The enemies peer into the camps of the Souljahs searching for ways to bring them down,
Hearing Souljahs chant, *"Fight the Power"* they seek out the weakest, to bring them down,
And they offer the weakest thirty pieces of silver to become a clown, to bring them down,
Is there a better way to bring a Souljah down than to make a Souljah into a foolish clown?

When they turn down the points on the crown,
The crown becomes the silly hat of a foolish clown,
And when they turn up the points on the hat of a clown,
Then the hat of the clown becomes the symbol of the crown,
And the clown who performed so well in the crown of the clown,
Still wearing the "inverted" crown of a clown on the head of a clown,
The enemies of the crown prop up the clown and pronounce the clown,
Officially pronouncing and crowning that clown to be the "King" of the clowns!

"Mustafa Rasul Al-Amin"
(Monday July 14, 2008)

"Habitual Rituals"
(Black Murders)

The murdering of young Afrikan men in AmeriKKKa, is acknowledged as predictable, habitual rituals,
Acceptable habitual rituals ingrained in predictable, dysfunctional behaviors, thought to be cultural,
Acceptable habitual rituals, rooted in predictable, dysfunctional behaviors taught to be cultural,
Deceitful, dysfunctional behaviors, deliberately taught as cultural rituals; affect the youthful!

"Mustafa Rasul Al-Amin"
(Tuesday September 30, 2008)

"Hip-Hop Is Not a Culture"
(It's A Crime)

We told you that Negro was not a race,
And we told you that Negro was not a place,
We told you that the culture vultures were lying to your face,
The culture vultures lied to your face telling you that a Negro face reflects race.......

We told you that Afro was not a race,
And we told you that Afro was not a place,
We told you that the culture vultures were lying to your face,
The culture vultures lied to your face telling you that an Afro place reflects your race.......

We're telling you that hip-hop is a plan and not a culture,
We're telling you that hip-hop is a Caucasian fabrication of the culture vultures,
We're telling you that the vultures are untruthful to you about this artificial, sub-culture,
The culture vultures are again lying to your face to destroy your race with a counter culture......

The culture vultures done taught you that hip-hop is a culture,
And like always, you unquestionably believe the lies of the culture vultures,
Like so many times in the past, you readily submit to the falsehoods of the vultures,
Ignoring and despising our Afrikan cultures, created to protect you from the vultures' cultures...

"Time keeps on slipping, slipping, slipping, into the future......."
And as we watch time march forward,
Black people appear to be marching backwards,
And forwards, becomes backwards, and backwards, becomes afterwards; and

"It's too late baby, aw it's too late......."
And I digress, as Black people regress,
Making little or no progress,
Even in the manner in which they dress.......

Or*; "Is it just my imagination, once again, running away with me?"*
"Oh, is it just my imagination, running away with me?"

And;
Black people seem to have an inherent inclination and an abnormal determination,
Coupled with an irrational fascination, when it comes to their voluntary participation,
And complete cooperation in detrimental situations that involve their own incarceration....

Or;
Could these manifestations of psychological devastations, be caused by the racial manipulations,
Daily instigated by, racist Caucasians in racist nations, reinforced by wicked "nigger" incantations,
Which, make Black people long for White subjugation, and cry out, to the return to the plantations,
And scream out for the plantations, and shout out for the places that profit from their incarceration,
As penitentiaries, prisons, jails, and places of incarcerations, become Massas' newest plantations?

Or*; "Is it just my imagination, once again, running away with me?"*
"Oh is it just my imagination, running away with me?"

And Hip-Hop routinely becomes just another COINTELPRO manipulation,
And another machination for African incarceration, devastation and extermination!

"Mustafa Rasul Al-Amin"
(Sunday April, 8 2007)

(Chapter Nine)

By most accounts the Willie Lynch tale is in truth an allegorical delineation based upon actual historical actions. Even so, there are life lessons to be learned from this allegory.

"CONTROLLING SLAVES"
(A Speech By William Lynch in 1712)

Gentlemen, I greet you here on the bank of the James River in the year of our Lord one thousand seven hundred and twelve. First, I shall thank you, the gentlemen of the Colony of Virginia, for bringing me here. I am here to help you solve some of your problems with slaves. Your invitation reached me on my modest plantation in the West Indies where I have experimented with some of the newest and still the oldest methods for control of slaves. Ancient Rome would envy us if my program is implemented.

As our boat sailed south on the James River, names for our illustrious King, whose version of the Bible we cherish, I saw enough to know that your problem is not unique. While Rome used cords of wood as crosses for standing human bodies along its old highways in great numbers you are here using the tree and the rope on occasion.

I caught the whiff of a dead slave hanging from a tree a couple of miles back. You are not only losing valuable stock by hangings, you are having uprisings, and slaves are running away, your crops are sometimes left in the fields too long for maximum profit, you suffer occasionally fires, and your animals are killed. Gentlemen, you know what your problems are. I do not need elaborate. I am not here to enumerate your problems; I am here to introduce you to a method of solving them.

In my bag here, I have a fool proof method for controlling your Black slaves. I guarantee every one of you that if installed correctly, it will control the slaves for at least 300 years. My method is simple. Any member of your family or your overseer can use it. I have outlined a number of differences among the slaves: and I take these differences and make them bigger. I use fear, distrust, and envy for control purposes. These methods have worked on my modest plantation in the West Indies and it will work throughout the South.

Take this simple little list of differences, and think about them. On top of my list is "Age" but it is only there because it starts with an "A": the second is "Color" or shade, there is intelligence, size, sex, size of plantations, status on plantation, attitude of owners, whether the slaves live in the valley, or on a hill, East, West, North, South, have fine hair or coarse hair, or is tall or short.

Now that you have a list of difference, I shall give you an outline of action, but before that I shall assure you that distrust is stronger that trust, and envy is stronger than adulation, respect and admiration. The Black slave after receiving this indoctrination shall carry on and will become self re-fueling and self generating for hundreds of years, maybe thousands.

Don't forget you must pitch the old Black male versus the young Black male and the young Black male against the old Black male. You must have the dark skin slaves versus the light skin slaves and the light skin slaves versus the dark skin slaves. You must use the female versus the male, and the male versus the female. You must also have your White servants and overseers distrust all Blacks, but it is necessary that your slaves trust and depend on us. They must love, respect and trust only us.

Gentlemen, these kits are your keys to control. Use them. Have your wives and children use them, never miss an opportunity. If used intensely for one year, the slaves themselves will remain perpetually distrustful. In other words, break their will to resist.

Now the breaking process is the same for both the horse and the nigger, only slightly varying in degree. But as we said before, there is an art to long range economic planning. You must keep your eye and thoughts on the female and the offspring of the horse and the nigger.

A brief discourse in offspring development will light on the key to sound principles. Pay little attention to the generation of original breaking but concentrate on future generations. Therefore, if you break the female mother, she will break the offspring in its early years of development and, when the offspring is old enough to work, she will it up to you for her normal female protective tendencies will have been lost in the original breaking process.

For example, take the case of the wild stud horse, a female and an already infant horse and compare the breaking process two captured nigger males in their natural state, a pregnant nigger woman with her infant offspring. Take the stud horse, break him for limited containment. Completely break the female horse until she becomes very gentle whereas you or anybody can ride her in comfort.

Breed the mare and the stud until you have the desired offspring. Then you can turn the stud to freedom until you need him again. Train the female horse whereby she will eat out of your hand, and she will, in turn, train the infant horse to eat out of your hand also.

When it comes to breaking the uncivilized nigger, use the same process, but vary the degree and step up the pressures so as to do a complete reversal of he mind. Take the meanest and most restless nigger, strip him of his clothes in front of the remaining male niggers, the female, and the nigger infant. Tar and feather him, tie each leg to a different horse faced in opposite directions, set him afire and beat both horses to pull him apart in front of the remaining nigger.

The next step is to take a bull whip and beat the remaining nigger male to the point of death in front of the female and the infant. Don't kill him, but put the fear of God in him, for he can be useful for future breeding.

Five Brothers hanged in Kentucky during a picnic and made into a postcard!

The Breaking Process Of The African Woman:

Then take the female, run a series of tests on her to see if she will submit to your desires willingly. Test her in every way because she is the most important factor for good economics. If she shows any sign of resistance in submitting completely to your will, do not hesitate to use the bull whip on her to extract that last bit of bitch out of her. Take care not to kill her, for in doing so, you spoil good economics. When in complete submission, she will train her off-spring in the early years to submit to labor when they come of age.

Understanding is the best thing. Therefore, we shall go deeper into the area of subject matter concerning what we have produced here in this breaking process of the female nigger. We have reversed the relationships. In her natural uncivilized state, she would have a strong dependency on the uncivilized nigger male and she would have a limited protective tendency toward her independent male offspring, and would raise the female offspring to be dependent like her. Nature had provided for this type of balance.

We reverse nature by burning, and pulling one uncivilized nigger apart and bull whipping the other to the point of death, all in her presence. By her being left alone, unprotected, with the male image destroyed, the ordeal caused her to move from her psychological dependent state to a frozen independent state. In this frozen psychological state of independence she will raise her male and female offspring in reversed roles.

For fear of the young male's life, she will psychologically train him to be mentally weak and dependent but physically strong. Because she has become psychologically independent, she will train her female offspring to be psychologically independent. What have you got? You've got the nigger woman out front and the nigger man behind and scared. This is a perfect situation for sound sleep and economics.

Before the breaking point, we had to be alertly on guard at all times. Now we can sleep soundly, for, out of frozen fear, his woman stands guard for us. He cannot get past her early infant slave molding process. He is a good tool, now ready to be tied to the horse at a tender age. By the time a nigger reaches the age of sixteen, he is soundly broken in and ready for a long life of sound and efficient work and the reproduction of a unit of good labor force.

Continually, through the breaking of uncivilized savage niggers, by throwing the nigger female savage into a frozen psychological state of independence, by the killing of the protective male image, and by creating a submissive dependent mind of the male nigger savage, we have created an orbiting cycle that turns on its own axis forever, unless a phenomenon occurs and re-shifts the positions of the male and female savages. We show what we meant by example, that the case of the two economic slave units and examine them closely.

A scene from Hollywood's big hit, "Birth Of A Nation"

The Negro Marriage Unit:

We breed the two nigger males with two nigger females. Then we take the nigger males away from them and keep them moving and working. Say the one nigger female bears a nigger female and the other bears a nigger male. Both nigger females, being without the influence of the nigger male image, frozen with an independent psychology, will raise their offspring into reverse positions. The one with the female offspring will teach her to be like herself, independent and negotiable (we negotiates with her, through her and by her, negotiate her at will).

The one with the nigger male offspring, she being frozen with a subconscious fear for his life, will raise him to be mentally dependent and weak but physically strong, in other words body over mind. Now in a few years when these two offspring become fertile for early reproduction, we will mate and breed them and continue the cycle. That is good, sound, and long range comprehensive planning.

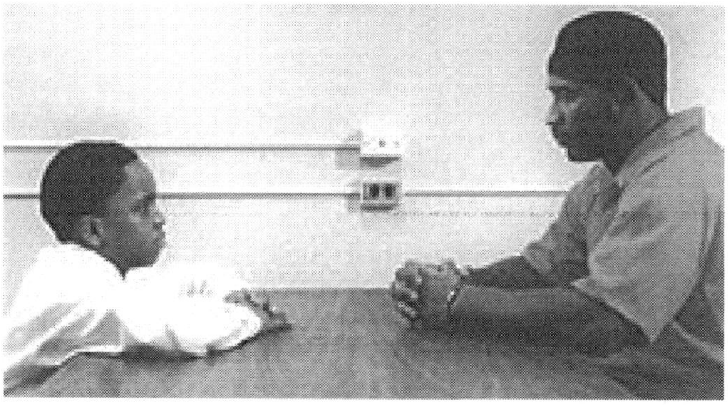

A large percentage of all Black Fathers are incarcerated or in the penal system

Warning: Possible Interloping Negatives:

Earlier we talked about the non-economic good of the horse and the nigger in their wild or natural state; we talked out the principle of breaking and tying them together for orderly production; furthermore, we talked about paying particular attention to the female savage and her offspring for orderly future planning; then more recently we stated that by, reversing the positions of the male and the female savages, we had created an orbiting cycle that turns on its own axis forever, unless phenomenon occurred and re-shifted the positions of the male and the female savages.

Our experts warned us about the possibility of this phenomenon occurring, for they say that the mind has a strong drive to correct and re-correct itself over a period of time if it can touch some substantial original historical base: and they advised us that the best way to deal with this phenomenon is to shave off the brute's mental history and create a multiplicity of phenomena of illusions, so that each illusion will twirl in its own orbit, something similar to floating balls in a vacuum.

This creation of multiplicity of phenomena of illusions entails the principles of cross-breeding the nigger and the horse as we stated above, the purpose of which is to create a diversified division of labor thereby creating different levels of labor and different values of illusion at each connecting level of labor, the results of which is the severance of the points of original beginnings for each sphere illusion.

Since we feel that the subject matter may get more complicated as we proceed in laying down our economic plan concerning the purpose, reason and effect of cross-breeding horses and niggers, we shall lay down the following definitional terms for future generations:

1. Orbiting cycle means a thing turning in a given path.

2. Axis means upon which or around which a body turns.

3. Phenomenon means something beyond ordinary conception and inspires awe and wonder.

4. Multiplicity means a great number.

5. Sphere means globe.

6. Cross-breeding a horse means taking a horse and breeding it with an ass and you get a dumb, backward ass, long headed mule that is neither reproductive nor productive by itself.

7. Cross-breeding niggers means taking so many drops of good white blood and putting them into as many nigger women as possible, varying the drops by the various tones that you want, and then breed with each other until the circle of colors appear as you desire.

What this means is this: Put the niggers and the horses in the same breeding pot, mix some asses and some good white blood and what do you get? You get a multiplicity of colors of ass backward, unusual niggers, running, tied to backward ass long headed mules, the one productive of itself, the other sterile, the one constant, the other dying. We keep the nigger constant for we may replace the mule for another tool. Both mule and nigger tied to each other, neither knowing where the other came from and neither productive for itself, nor without each other.

This humble man was hung right after church simply because of the color of his skin

Controlled Language:

Cross-breeding completed, for further severance from their original beginning, we must completely annihilate the mother tongue of both the new nigger and the new mule and institute a new language that involves the new life's work for both.

You know, language is a peculiar institution. It leads to the heart of a people. The more a foreigner knows about the language of another country the more he is able to move through all levels of that society. Therefore, if the foreigner is an enemy of another country, to the extent that he knows the body of the language, to that extent is the country vulnerable to attack or invasion of a foreign culture.

For example, you take a slave, if you teach him all about your language, he will know all your secrets, and he is then no more a slave, for you can't fool him any longer, and being a fool is one of the basic ingredients of and incidents to the maintenance of this slavery system.

For example, if you told a slave that he must perform in getting out "our crops" and he knows the language well, he would know that "our crops," didn't mean "our crops," and the slavery system would break down, for he would relate on the basis of what "our crops" really meant. So you have to be careful in setting up the new language, for the slave would soon be in your house, talking to you as "man to man" and that is death to our economic system. In addition, the definitions of the words or terms are only a minute part of the process. Values are created and transported by communication through the body of the language. A total society has many inter-connected value systems.

All these values in the society have bridges of language to connect them for orderly workings in the society. But for these language bridges, these many value systems would sharply clash and cause internal strife or civil war, the degree of the conflict being determined by the magnitude of the issues or relative opposing strength in whatever form.

For example, if you put a slave in a hog pen and train him to live there and incorporate in him to value it as a way of life completely, the biggest problem you would have out of him is that he would worry you about provisions to keep that hog pen clean, or partially clean, or he might not worry you at all. On the other hand, if you put this same slave in the same hog pen and make a slip and incorporate something in his language whereby he comes to value a horse more than he does his hog pen, you got a problem. He will soon be in your house. Thank you gentlemen.

Chapter Ten

Conclusion

(Solutions)

Al-Quran Surah 96 Ayats 1 through 5;

1. *Read in the name of thy Lord who creates*
2. *Creates man from a clot,*
3. *Read and thy Lord is most generous,*
4. *Who taught by the pen,*
5. *Taught man what he knew not.*

Frequently, we read books which critique and criticize Afrikan-American people and our communities; and in the end, they offer no viable solutions to the many problems and situations, which they so eagerly pass judgments upon. So many people appear to be relentlessly searching for those answers to the countless trials and tribulations facing Black people today. Continuously, far too many people presuppose that, the solutions to our predicaments can be readily solved by tossing money and Jesus (religion) at them. They constantly invent program after program, which are usually based on religious principles and foundations; accumulating, and squandering so much money. Why can't people understand that, if hurling money and religion at all our problems could solve all our problems; then long ago many of our problems would have been resolved?

Money and religions are not the solutions to the numerous of problems which daily affect and effect Black people. In fact many of our hardships stem from; blindly submitting to those fictitious cultures in which the enslavers of Afrikan people have produced, and publicized, especially for the Afrikans' demise. When we become so caught up in counterfeit cultures, which are premeditated to, reinvent, and reconstruct Afrikan peoples, transforming Afrikans into niggers; we are in actual fact, surrendering to the racists. Money and religions are fundamentally, nothing more than tools, utilized by the racists, to indoctrinate unconstructive emotions deep inside us; filling Afrikans with the unenthusiastic, and uncooperative beliefs of envy, greed, lust, hatred, individualism and materialism, which are instilled in us for the purposes of destroying us.

If Afrikans are going to survive and thrive as a people, they must be enthusiastic about, bringing about the intellectual and psychological changes necessary for the survival of Afrikan peoples. Afrikans ought to be willing to change our ways of thinking. Our changes cannot be changes of insincerity, which momentarily satisfy selfish, self-centered egos. Our changes cannot be based on, or exist upon, monetarily motivated or deceptive religious, and cultural foundations. It is for these reasons we say, "Money and religion is not the solution to Afrikan problems!" The Afrikans' problems are behavioral in nature. This is the reason; we have got to change our ways thinking, and correct our psychological and sociological behavioral patterns. It is just that simple people.

Although niggers are actual, tangible, touchable creations, they are still the wicked inventions of iniquitous imaginations, produced by transforming Afrikans' thought processes. None is inherently a nigger. This is no mysterious, inexplicable phenomenon. Niggers are taught to be niggers! Niggers are daily taught how to function like niggers, how to speak like niggers, how to act like niggers, how to believe like niggers, and how to believe in niggers; to become niggers.

Continually bombarded with disadvantageous nigger images on television, in movies, in video games and on the printed pages; Black people are continually being brainwashed, and cast into those nigger roles, to become niggers. Furthermore, day after day, the racists acclimatize Afrikan children; to be a detriment to themselves and their communities, through the utilization of wicked, misrepresented, demonic drumbeats and wicked, satanically distorted drum calls. The malevolent racists purposely pervert Afrikan drumbeats and interweave them into the gangsta rap beats of a *bogus*, media-created, hip-hop culture, premeditated to transform Afrikan men, women and children into their pathetically apathetic, dysfunctional, *pet niggers.*

The solutions to Afrikans' problems are psychological in nature, and accordingly demand changes in our ways of thinking. Ignorance is the Afrikan's greatest adversary and apathy its greatest ally. To come up out of our oppression we must begin utilizing our thinking processes in coherent and advantageous ways. When we begin to coherently think, we begin to understand that money, and religions, which were forced upon us, are the reasons that we are in many of the predicaments, and situations in which we now suffer.

As many of us have now come to understand, it was necessary to alter Afrikans psychologically to ensure the complete and total enslavement of Afrikans; mentally, physically and spiritually (mind, body and soul). Afrikans are a people, kidnapped from their Ancestral lands, enslaved in the lands of their oppressors and (ignorantly) let loose into strange societies and cultures as amnesiacs; with no idea of who we are or from whence we came. Afrikans are a people which endured the hellacious tortures of chattel slavery; abused unremittingly in the most horrifying of ways and then let loose in an uncompromisingly hostile and abusive society, without benefit of psychological therapy or psychological counsel. Upon release from internment, Afrikans were commanded to never question the authority or the motives of their enslavers. It is for these reasons we must begin inquiring about the motives and the authority, of the oppressors of Afrikan people.

We have an obligation to take back our minds, reestablish our cultures and destroy all the negative things that give rise to niggers. We are ethically obligated to save our children. It is our Godly requirement, that we rescue, revive and resuscitate the minds of our people. It is essential that we recognize, acknowledge and understand situations and circumstances of detriment; and that we commence to instigate campaigns of destruction against all things which have been premeditatedly designed to destroy Afrikans.

Misunderstanding, misinformation, misrepresentation, miseduKKKation and instructions from the *Creator* are the events that led to the idea for and the creation of this book. This book had to be written, because so many oppressed peoples, so many of my people, of which, whom I love so dearly, because they have no real knowledge of the things that they submit to; they suffer and perish. Knowing this, our oppressors, the representatives of our oppressors, and now victims of our oppressors spew forth the bigots' rhetorical, racial confusions with a venomous passion, and we must stop this with the intention of saving our people!

Armed with their well learned, well rehearsed, messages of oppressive racial rhetoric, our oppressors and their agents have besieged our loving, but *uninformed* people, with duplicitous campaigns of propaganda for the purposes of subjugating and exploiting them for their own avaricious benefit. They have launched coercive campaigns of confusion and fright. The utilization and exploitation of fear and intimidation; with the use of superstitions, false cultures and peer pressure, under the guise of recruiting souls (soldiers) for their army of God (Jesus); they daily conquer the hearts, minds and souls of our beleaguered people!

Knowing that our people possess no accurate knowledge of themselves, or their unequaled Afrikan pasts, they are continuously deceived, routinely chastised, deliberately persecuted, purposefully psychologically re-eduKKKated, knowingly sociologically redefined, spiritually Christianized, and absolutely dehumanized; by those very same *terrorists* that diminish and curse Afrikans, with the racist White religions and religious teachings that promulgate and sustain White supremacy, which they are being recruited into!

So, you see, me having love for the people; this book had to be written and is written to raise the levels of consciousness and awareness which is being consciously and intentionally suppressed within oppressed people everywhere; and me being Afrikan, it is especially written as a defensive tool, for Afrikan Souljahs!

Afrikan Unity

Continually, we hear calls of unity being issued amongst Black people and throughout Black communities. Unfortunately, these disingenuous calls of unity; continuously fall upon unresponsive ears, unsympathetic hearts and apathetic souls. The unity that we all seem to crave, and need so much, proves to be nothing more than manifestations of vaporous dreams and fabricated manipulations; invented for the subjugation of Afrikan populations. I say disingenuous, because more often than not, their calls for unity are not real. Vaporous dreams; because the foundations for the unanimity which we seek are daily disintegrating and fast becoming non-existent, wishful dreams. There can be no Afrikan liberty with out Afrikan unity.

When even the unanimity of our families, those bonds of trust, commitment, and collaboration among our parents, siblings, and relatives are so fragile that they often appear non-existent; then how can we expect to ever bring about the unity necessary, to right us, and strengthen us as a people? Increasingly, it is our families which hold us back and give us the smallest amounts of the fundamental support and assistance which is often needed to complete our *divinely* assigned tasks. There can be no liberty with out unity.

The Sermon Of The Mother And Brethren

While yet he talked to the people, behold, his mother and his brethren stood without, desiring to speak with him. Then one said unto him, Behold, thy mother and thy brethren stand without, desiring to speak with thee. But he answered and said unto him that told him, "Who is my mother? And who are my brethren?" And he stretched forth his hand toward his disciples, and said, "Behold my mother and my brethren!" For whosoever shall do the will of my Father which is in heaven, the same is my mother, and sister, and brother.

Matthew 12 verses 46 through 50

Learn These Lessons Well

Please learn from this book, be empowered by this book and accept these lessons from this book as an aid in our confrontation against our oppressors utilizing, *"Religion, Deception, Science and the Truth!"*

More and more, jails and prisons are fast becoming illogical rites of passage for Black males and females, as far too many foolishly begin to equate Blackness with incarceration; and real nigger-ism is ridiculously being embraced as virtuous, and we all know that, *"Real niggers go to jail!"* Consequently, my real niggas are programmed to fail, to go to jail; to strengthen and feed the voracious appetites of the prison industrial complex. Kill the mind and the body and soul will fall victim to an eternally agonizing oppressive death.

In Black communities, jails and penitentiaries are rapidly becoming the most influential institutions, which affect Black communities. Penitentiaries daily affect, influence and pervert the consciousnesses of Black people. The behaviors of Black people, the articulations of Black people, the fashionable trends of Black people, the principles of Black people, the ideologies of Black people, the ethicalness of Black people and the religions, and spiritual consciousnesses of Black people are all influenced by incarcerated mentalities. Essentially, jails and penitentiaries are rapidly turning into the criminal colleges and the iniquitous spiritual centers of Black communities; offering its graduates degrees in criminalization, and wicked consecrations and ordinations based in and based upon systemic discombobulations; succumbing to beliefs of thug-ism.

The most significant dilemma that Black people encounter, and daily suffer from, is their own inability and refusals to recognize, understand and accept truth. Daily imprisoned by lies, bombarded with lies, and so saturated in those lies, until the total embodiment of their existences become completely dependent upon the lies of the racists, and the misinformed misconceptions of their own brethren.

As a people, we see the problems but refuse to acknowledge the problems, we refuse take the necessary or appropriate actions to combat or even take a stand against those problems, or we continually refuse to take responsibility for the consequences of ignoring those problems. On some existential level, all Black people recognize the differences between Black people of consciousness, and niggers. We know what a nigger is, we know how niggers act, we know who those niggers are, and on many levels we all know that niggers are repugnantly disadvantageous to the futures, of all Afrikan people. That is why so many Black people frequently say, *"Stop acting like them niggers!"* Niggers are detrimental to everything Afrikan.

We know niggers exist, but we indefatigably deny their existence, or we fail to recognize, or acknowledge the existences of them. We know niggers exist! However, in the public arena, most of us daily challenge the factuality of niggers, whilst simultaneously condoning, defending, justifying, and even supporting their contemptible, nigger-like actions. Niggers do exist and we need to learn how to confront them in order to destroy them. Niggers are resultant of an intentionally inflicted (psychological) mental illness (injury).

Many in the unsympathetic society of the racists' have found an unconscionable benefit, and a somewhat perverse prosperity and profitability, in Afrikan suffering. They thrive on Black suffering as Black suffering generates enormous economic rewards, for those most skilled in the art fleecing the impoverished Afrikan masses. The pulpits of many Black churches produce numerous Black millionaires; exploiting Black pain.

Not trying to sound cliché, or rhetorical but, do you ever openly ask, "Why are there so many liquor stores and churches on nearly every corner in Black communities? Why are there so many Black organizations, and so many helpless, stationary, community action groups in Black communities? Furthermore, why are there now so many are unemployed, so-called community activists (freshly released from the penitentiary) suddenly popping up at such an unrestrained pace? Finally, why do you think they are building so many new jails in White communities; for the incarceration of Afrikans?"

It's big business baby! Unfortunately, it has been just like this since the beginning. Their big business is your Black Ass! Those venues of incarceration, churches, liquor stores, check cashing places, blood and plasma donor centers, and a host of other enterprises; are all extremely lucrative businesses. These are commercial interests, which prey on Afrikans and sustain the interests of Caucasians economically, while buttressing the ideologies of racism and White supremacy. Can you say, "Parasitical political racists?"

Self anointed, White appointed, Black activists are the newest set of predators who pray their way into the hearts of their hapless, hopeless Black prey. They profit from Black pain. The undertakings of these self-centered, egotistical, predatory representatives are not intended to remove the problems of Black people. Black people and Black anguish is their job security, and Black suffering is the foundation of their income. In addition, the art of poetic speechifying is their method of achieving access to your Black purse strings.

Niggers were purposefully created and placed in this society to be economically beneficial to some and to be economic commodities for others. Many view niggers as manufactured goods and items for economic consumption. As it was in the past, they refuse to see our humanity, or our humanness. To this day, the racists still view Blacks as chattel and as very little more than their beasts of burden. To the racists, Black bodies are commodities.

One major realization that each Afrikan upon this Earth must come to realize is that, the racist adversaries have instigated every characteristic of war, against all people of Afrikan descent. The racists' subterfuges have always been to cripple, control and kill Afrikans psychologically, religiously, socially, and physically, "By Any Means Necessary!" All Afrikans must begin to understand, and acknowledge the realization that a highly organized, sophisticated and intricately devised system of racist genocide has been, and is being implemented, and orchestrated against all Afrikan people. Afrikan People, when are we going to wake up and smell the genocide?

The problem is, we are in a war, and far too many of us don't even know it and too many of us don't even care. Afrikan people are being exterminated on holocaustic levels in a war they declared on Black People eons ago. Afrikans are in a war that for the most part, is being unnoticed by us. Afrikan people, for some ridiculous reason don't realize, or don't want to understand that a declaration of war has been imposed on them and this war is being fought against them, with or without their participation or cooperation.

As I conclude this book, I make an effort to conclude it with information and instructions, which will guide and keep my children, and my people onto the path of righteousness, information, and coherent thinking. I have attempted to write from the perspective of, "What I wish I knew when I was younger," in an effort to turn the readers away from the ignorant mistakes that I have made in this life. With any luck this averting will save the reader from many of the mistakes, heartaches, and hardships that I have had to endure.

"Mustafa Rasul Al-Amin"

"I have given them all I know! "

"Marcus Moshia Garvey"
(Detroit 1937)

"BENDERA"

(Our Flag: The Red The Black And The Green)

Oh mighty Bendera symbol of Afrikan Unity,
We stand before The Bendera to show the world our Afrikan identity!
Oh mighty Bendera symbol of Afrikan identity,
We stand before The Bendera to show the world our Afrikan Unity!

"One God, One Aim, One Destiny!"
As every nation proudly display their flags that they may be seen,
We proudly raise and display the Red, the Black, And the Green...........
The oldest national colors known to man,
These are the ancient colors of the Afrikan,
Colors that go back to the Zinj Empires of ancient Afrika,
Existing thousands of years before Greece, Rome, France, England or America!

At the top of all things stands the Red or the Blood...........
We lost our land through the Blood, and cannot regain it except through the Blood!
We lost our lives through the Blood, and must redeem our lives through the Blood,
Even if the price of redemption calls for the shedding of Blood!

"One God, One Aim, One Destiny!"
Since we can't go forward if we don't look back.......
The Black stands meaningfully in the center tract,
As millions of years back the first humans were created Black,
Born Black and created Black in Afrika's the center tract,
The Mothers and Fathers of all humanity were created Black,
In Ethiopia and Tanzania at Olduvai Gorge the human was created Black,
Afrika's center tract!

"One God, One Aim, One Destiny!"
The Green represents the Land...........
Lands fertile, rich and stolen from The Afrikan,
Lands the world over which is denied The Afrikan,
Lands that could bring freedom, justice, independence, and equality to The Afrikan,
Lands necessary for The African, to be The Afrikan!

"One God, One Aim, One Destiny!"
Reestablished in 1920 as the banner of the United Negro Improvement Association,
Marcus Moshia Garvey resurrected these ancient colors to heal all Afrikan Nations!

We thank you Brother Marcus for the resurrection!
We thank you Brother Marcus for the recollection!
We thank you Brother Marcus for the connection!
We thank you Brother Marcus for the reflection!
We thank you Brother Marcus for the direction!

Oh mighty Bendera symbol of Afrikan Unity,
We stand before The Bendera to show the world our Afrikan identity!
Oh mighty Bendera symbol of Afrikan identity,
We stand before The Bendera to show the world our Afrikan Unity!

"One God, One Aim, One Destiny!

"Mustafa Rasul Al-Amin"
(111896)

"Distress Signal"
(From the Last Souljah Left)

I,
Stand in the middle of a Battlefield,
Of,
Unconscious people,
Who,
Dream that they are conscious,
And,
They dream numinous dreams,
Of,
Harmonious, mythological Afrikan peoples and villages,
Dreaming those numinous dreams,
Of,
Mythological,
Supernatural peoples with Black consciences,
And,
They sleep walk,
Through a noticeably conscienceless world,
In various states of unconsciousness,
Obstinately claiming to be,
And cleverly disguised as,
Souljahs,
Donning the sheep's wool,
They impersonate Souljahs of truth,
They impersonate Souljahs of awareness,
They impersonate Souljahs of consciousness!

I,
Stand in the middle of a Battlefield,
Of,
Unconscious people,
And,
I'm only just now realizing,
That I'm the last Souljah left,
For,
I see different battles when it comes to the fight,
Pertaining to wrong and right,
I view our enemies under a different light,
I watch as the oppressors blind a Black nation and steal their sight,

I,
Stand in the middle of a Battlefield,
Of unconscious people,
Realizing that I'm the last Souljah left,
And;
I'm sending a distress signal to any other Souljah that may be left!

I'm the last Souljah left.......

"Mustafa Rasul Al-Amin"
(Friday January 11, 2008)

"Osagyefo"

(The Twi Word Meaning Redeemer or Savior)

When we speak the name Osagyefo, we pay homage to an Afrikan Redeemer,
When we speak the name Osagyefo, we call upon the name of an Afrikan Savior,
When we speak the name Osagyefo, we articulate Twi to praise an Afrikan warrior,
When we speak the name Osagyefo, we demonstrate respect for an Afrikan Souljah!

Majestic warrior anointed by The Divine Creator to be a Redeemer and Savior of Afrikan nations,
Ever vigilant in a Divine occupation our Afrikan warrior of Divine ordination is always on station,
Divine elevation from foundations in perceived common stations, are truly Divine proclamations,
Without vacillation Osagyefo answered the Divine proclamation of ordination without hesitation!

When we speak the name Osagyefo, we pay homage to an Afrikan Redeemer,
When we speak the name Osagyefo, we call upon the name of an Afrikan Savior,
When we speak the name Osagyefo, we articulate Twi to praise an Afrikan warrior,
When we speak the name Osagyefo, we demonstrate respect for an Afrikan Souljah!

Oh magnificent Redeemer of Afrikan liberation and uncompromising Savior of Afrikan salvation,
Cautionary Elder warning the masses about the ills of oppression, occupation and incarceration,
Perpetually vigilant against causations of Black consternation our Redeemer fights for liberation,
Marching against oppressive soldiers of occupation our Savior battles for the Afrikan's salvation!

When we speak the name Osagyefo, we pay homage to an Afrikan Redeemer,
When we speak the name Osagyefo, we call upon the name of an Afrikan Savior,
When we speak the name Osagyefo, we articulate Twi to praise an Afrikan warrior,
When we speak the name Osagyefo, we demonstrate respect for an Afrikan Souljah!

Armed with historical demonstrations, Divine narrations, and crucial contemporary information,
The dissemination of information became your vocation and we witnessed your Divine orations,
Divine orations coupled with wise narrations and boisterous proclamations, inspire generations,
Divine orations and spiritual narrations that transcends the boundaries of TV and radio stations!

When we speak the name Osagyefo, we pay homage to an Afrikan Redeemer,
When we speak the name Osagyefo, we call upon the name of an Afrikan Savior,
When we speak the name Osagyefo, we articulate Twi to praise an Afrikan warrior,
When we speak the name Osagyefo, we demonstrate respect for an Afrikan Souljah!

When Souljahs look at a book, our imaginations are sparked by your inspiration and dedication,
When Souljahs look to Osagyefo consternation become anticipations of optimistic expectations,
When Souljahs speak the name Osagyefo we summons his courage for our spiritual fortification,
When Souljahs speak the name Osagyefo we rely upon his strength to empower Afrikan nations!

I call upon the name of Osagyefo and summon the spirits of Divine Souljahs!
I call upon the name of Osagyefo and summon the spirits of Divine Warriors!
I call upon the name of Osagyefo and summon the spirits of Divine Redeemers!
I call upon the name of Osagyefo and summon the spirits of the greatest Saviors!

Osagyefo the Souljah routinely walks among us and no one appears to recognize his ordination,
Osagyefo the Warrior, constantly warns about subjugation and no one recognizes his divination,
Osagyefo the Redeemer, is tasked with the dissemination of information for Afrikan reclamation,
Osagyefo the Savior unpretentiously strolls amongst us, as commanded by Divine proclamation!

"Mustafa Rasul Al-Amin"
(Wednesday August 28, 2009)

"MAMMA I SAW MONSTERS!"

(White Skin, Thin Nose, Thin Hair, Blue-Eyed Demons)

Run! Run little one run!
For Shaitan has come to Alkebu-lan,
And he has an appetite for the souls of the young ones,
Young African boy running through the woods,
Running from Shaitan as fast as he could,
If only the village had understood,
That the killing of devils is always good!

In 1796 a little African boy ran through the woods on African night,
With nostrils flared, hair tight and skin as Black as night,
When suddenly he came upon a horrible of demonic torture in the night,
And he stared into a demonic night by the light of the demons camp site,
Witnessing shrill screams and evil, satanic sights of fright,
And hearing the devilish laughter of demons whose skin was White,
Satanic sights and sounds that pierced the quiet tranquility of the African night!

And as the little African boy ran through the night,
Screaming for his Mother to ease his fright,
She held him tight as he told his story of fright,
Shivering and shaking in the heat of an African night...........

What did they look like?

They looked like men,
Men with no color in their skin,
Men with hair, noses, and lips which were thin,
Men with evil hearts and demonic blue eyes full of sin,
Demonic men who delight in the peeling of African skin!

Two weeks later while gathering wood from the woods,
The little African Brother ventured out just as he should,
In an effort to find the best wood that he could,
When he saw the White skinned demons in the woods,
Demons in the woods trapping children in the woods,
And the little one ran as fast as he could,
But all his running did him no good,
As the demons snatched him from the woods!

Run! Run little one run!
For Shaitan has come to Alkebu-lan,
And he has an appetite for the souls of the young ones,
Young African boy running through the woods,
Running from Shaitan as fast as he could,
If only the village had understood,
That the killing of devils is always good!

In 1796 a thirteen year-old boy was kidnapped from the West Coast of Africa,
Chained to the bottom of a slave ship for 3 1/2 months and brought to AmeriKKKa,
With nostrils flared, hair tight and skin as Black as night,
He fell asleep one demonic night and woke up in a hellish plight,
And the little African Brother would never again see his Mother...........
Run! Run little one run!

For Shaitan has come to Alkebu-lan,
And he has an appetite for the souls of the young ones,

Young African girl running through the woods,
Running from Shaitan as fast as she could,
If only the village had understood,
That the killing of devils is always good!

In 1796 a little African girl ran through the night, in fright on an African night,
With nostrils flared, hair tight and skin as Black as night,
She stares into a demonic night by the light of a camp site,
Witnessing and experiencing shrill screams and satanic sights of fright,
Whilst enduring the devilish laughter of demons whose skin was White,
Satanic sights and sounds that pierced the quiet tranquility of the African night!

Run! Run little one run!
For Shaitan has come to Alkebu-lan,
And he has an appetite for the souls of the young ones,
Young African girl running through the woods,
Running from Shaitan as fast as she could,
If only the village had understood,
That the killing of devils is always good!

In 1796 a thirteen year-old girl was kidnapped from the West Coast of Africa,
Chained to the bottom of a slave ship for 3 1/2 months and brought to AmeriKKKa,
With nostrils flared, hair tight and skin as Black as night,
She fell asleep one demonic night and woke up in a hellish plight,
And the little African Sister would never again see her Mother...........

Repeatedly gang raped as White demons forcibly pierce her thighs and spit inside,
As demon after demon pierce her thighs, crawl inside, planting their seeds deep inside,
She longs to die!
Yet, chained so tight, she can't even attempt suicide, so she prays for a homicide,
As vicious White devils pierce her thighs and spray their evil White seeds deep inside!

In 1796 a thirteen year old African Mother-to-be arrived on the shores of AmeriKKKa,
A 13 year old rape victim, 3 1/2 months pregnant, stolen from the shores of Africa,
Whether it be from their racial embarrassment or strictly for the racists amusement,
A 13 year old rape victim and Mother-to-be, was about to be, their entertainment!

In thirteen degree weather,
In the Thirteen Colonies,
On the thirteenth day of December,
Stood a thirteen year old rape victim and African old Mother-to-be...........

Stripped, whipped, flipped and again whipped,
Baby Girl was hung by her ankles from a tree,
To the sounds of the demonic, White racist glee,
And repeatedly whipped as the temperatures dipped,
Our Baby girl was sliced open to just above her hip...........

Her baby falls out onto the ground,
As the White demonic demons make a joyful sound,
As the devil takes the heel of his boot and crushes the baby's head into the ground,
All those sick, demonic, White bitches and bastards dance sing and jump around,
Whilst Baby Girl and her baby girl lie naked, bloodied, and dead on the cold ground!

She ran through the night of an African night in fright,
Screaming for her Mother to ease her pain and her fright,
And as her mother held her tight,
She told the story of her plight,
Shivering and shaking in the heat of an African night...........

What did they look like?

They looked like men,
Men with no color in their skin,
Men with hair, noses, and lips which were thin,
Men with evil hearts and demonic blue eyes full of sin,
Demonic men who delight in the peeling of African skin!

And just before she closed her eyes and died...........
These were her last words uttered aloud to the crowd...........

Run! Run little one run!
For Shaitan has come to Alkebu-lan,
And he has an appetite for the souls of the young ones,
Young African child run through the woods,
Run from Shaitan as fast as you could,
If only the village had understood,
That the killing of devils is always good!

In 1796 on that very same day in that very same hour,
The little African boy was sold to the family of Powers,
To be brutalized, victimized, sodomized and lobotomized,
And just before he closed his eyes he found the strength to cry...........

In his mind, in his mind, in his mind,
The little African boy ran through the night,
Screaming for his Mother to ease his fright,
And as she held him tight he told the story of his plight,
Shivering and shaking in the heat of an African night...........

What did they look like?
They looked like men,
Men with no color in their skin,
Men with hair, noses, and lips which were thin,
Men with evil hearts and demonic blue eyes full of sin,
Demonic men who delight in the peeling of African skin!

And now their spirits ask me...........

Why do so many of you now hate yourselves,
And why do so many of you now view beauty,
As being like those White demons of the night?"

What did they look like?
They looked like men,
Men with no color in their skin.......

"Mustafa Rasul Al-Amin"
(112896)

"Untitled"

You must understand the knowledge and truth of things seemingly unperceived,
I'm trying to make you perceive the truth by insuring the information is received,
Understanding truth will protect you from those purposely keeping you deceived

Do you understand the words that are coming out of my mouth?
Do you understand the words from my mouth are from my soul?

"Mustafa Rasul Al-Amin"
(Sunday June 10, 2007)

"Niggers"
(Another Thought)

Niggers are the iniquitous souls of White men cloaked in Black skin.

"Mustafa Rasul Al-Amin"
(Sunday June 10, 2007)

One must never stop reading. Read everything that you can read that is a standard of knowledge. Don't waste time reading trashy literature.

"Marcus Moshia Garvey"

Seeking knowledge is hard, retaining it in memory is harder than seeking it, applying it is harder than retaining it in memory, and remaining safe from it is harder than applying it.
.... Hilal ibn 'Ala

"I have taught thee in the ways of wisdom; I have led thee in the right paths"

Proverbs 4; 11

"My People are destroyed for lack of knowledge"

Hosea 6; 4

John 8:32

And ye shall know the truth and the truth shall make you free.

Luke 12:2

For there is nothing covered, that shall not be revealed, neither hid, that shall not be known.

Al-'Alaq
(The Clot)

1. *Read in the Name of thy Lord Who creates;*
2. *Creates Man from a clot,*
3. *Read and thy Lord is most generous,*
4. *Who taught Man by pen,*
5. *Taught Man what he knew not.*

"Our Afrikan Pledge"

(Our Afrikan Pledge Of Unity And Oneness)

We are an Afrikan People!

We will regain our original spirituality and serve The Creator diligently!

We will remember the humanity, the glory, and the suffering of Our Ancestors!

We will honor the struggles of Our Elders and respect Our Elders!

We will strive to bring new values and new life to Our People!

We will have peace and harmony among us!

We will be a loving, sharing and creative People!

We will make the problems of one, the problems of all, and solve them together!

We will work, study, and listen, so we may learn, and learn, so we may teach!

We will cultivate Self reliance, building our own businesses and communities!

We will struggle to resurrect and unify Our Ancestral homeland!

We will create the village that it takes to raise the Child, to build the nation!

We will have love, unity, discipline, patience, devotion and courage!

We will live as Role Models to provide new directions for Our People!

We will listen to One Another and try to understand One Another!

We will be free, free thinking, and self-determining!

We will define ourselves, name ourselves, create for, and speak for ourselves!

We will strive to live by the principles of The Nguzo Saba!

We will study to learn our true history that Each One may teach one!

We will always seek the truth, espouse the truth, and expose untruthfulness!

We will forever remember that we are an Afrikan People!

Gye Nyame

Nguzo Saba
(Social And Spiritual Principles)

UMOJA (UNITY) (oo-MOE-jah) - To strive for and maintain unity in the family, the community, the nation and the race

KUJICHAGULIA (SELF DETERMINATION) (koo-jee-cha-goo-LEE-ah) - To define ourselves, name ourselves, create for ourselves and speak for ourselves

UJIMA (COLLECTIVE WORK AND RESPONSIBILITY) (oo-JEE-mah) - To build and maintain our community together and to make our brothers' and sisters' problems our problems and to solve them together

UJAMAA (COOPERATIVE ECONOMICS) (oo-JAH-mah) - To build and maintain our own stores, shops and other businesses and to profit together from them.

NIA (PURPOSE) (nee-AH) - To make as our collective vocation the building and developing of our community in order to restore our people to their traditional greatness

KUUMBA (CREATIVITY) (koo-OOM-bah) - To do always as much as we can, in the way that we can, in order to leave our community more beautiful and beneficial than when we inherited it

IMANI (FAITH) (ee-MAH-nee) - To believe with all our hearts in our people and the righteousness and victory of our struggle

86002946R00048

Made in the USA
Columbia, SC
23 December 2017